BRITISH LABOUR STRUGGLES:
CONTEMPORARY PAMPHLETS 1727-1850

REPEAL

OF

THE COMBINATION ACTS >

Five Pamphlets and One Broadside

1825

Arno Press

A New York Times Company/New York 1972

Reprint Edition 1972 by Arno Press Inc.

Reprinted from copies in the Kress Library
Graduate School of Business Administration,
Harvard University

The imperfections found in this edition
reflect defects in the originals which
could not be eliminated.

BRITISH LABOUR STRUGGLES: CONTEMPORARY PAMPHLETS 1727-1850
ISBN for complete set: 0-405-04410-0

See last pages for complete listing.

Manufactured in the United States of America

Library of Congress Cataloging in Publication Data
Main entry under title:

Repeal of the Combination Acts.

(British labour struggles:
contemporary pamphlets 1727-1850)
    CONTENTS: Rules and regulations, for the formation
of a society, to be called the United Association of
Colliers [first published 1825].--A voice from the coal
mines, by the colliers of the United Association of
Durham and Northumberland [first published 1825].--
Observations on the laws relating to the colliers in
Scotland [first published 1825]. [etc.]
    1. Trade-unions--Great Britain. I. Series.
LAW   344'.42'018   72-2540
ISBN 0-405-04432-1

Contents

RULES

AND

REGULATIONS,

FOR THE FORMATION OF A SOCIETY,

TO BE CALLED

THE UNITED

ASSOCIATION OF COLLIERS,

ON THE

RIVERS TYNE AND WEAR.

————•••••••••••••————

NEWCASTLE UPON TYNE:
PRINTED BY JOHN MARSHALL,
IN THE OLD FLESH-MARKET.
1825.

ARTICLES,

&c.

PREAMBLE

WE, the undersigned, being persons following the employment of Miners or Colliers, upon the rivers Tyne and Wear, Do, (by virtue of the several Acts of Parliament made and passed in the 33rd. year of the reign of his late Majesty, George III. c. 54 ; the 35th. year of the reign of his said late Majesty, c. 111 ; the 43rd. year of the said King's reign, c. 111 ; and the 49th. of the same reign, e. 125 ; and also the late Act of Parliament made and passed in the 6th. year of the reign of his present Majesty, c. 129 ; in order to enable persons to associate themselves together for making provision for themselves and families, in case of death, sickness, or other bodily infirmities ; and also to meet to obtain a fair and reasonable remuneration and payment for their labour, and to regulate the hours of labour ; being desirous of complying with the before mentioned Acts of Parliament, and the laws of this kingdom) agree to associate ourselves together, from the day of the date hereof, in order to make provision for ourselves and families, in cases of death, sickness, or other accidents or infirmities, and to unite in a firm manner, in order to obtain a more suitable recompense for our labour, and to regulate the hours of labour : And do therefore hereby voluntarily, for ourselves and for each and every of us, and for our and each and every of our several and respective heirs, executors, and administrators, bind ourselves well and truly to perform, fulfil, and keep the several Rules and Regulations hereinafter mentioned and contained, on each and every of our respective parts ; and which Rules and Regulations, Clauses and Agreements, are to the purport and effect following ; that is to say,—

ARTICLE I.

THAT this Society be established and permanently held in Newcastle upon Tyne, and be called and known by the name of " *The United Association of Colliers on the Rivers Tyne and Wear.*"

II.

That this Society be under the immediate management and controul of thirty-one Members, to be chosen out of the whole body of Members, and be known or called by the names of " *The General Committee or Guardians.*" Which said General Committee or Guardians shall, on the first Saturday in every month, meet at a proper place in Newcastle upon Tyne, to be selected by them, for the purpose of transacting the business of the said Society; and that such Committee or Guardians have full power and authority, and the same is hereby vested in them and their successors, to appoint a proper person or persons to act as the Clerk or Clerks to the said Society, and to appoint all such other officers as to the said Committee or Guardians shall seem meet for the better management of the same; and shall also fix the salaries to be paid to the said persons so to be appointed as aforesaid; and that such General Committee or Guardians continue stationary for one year and no more, when a new General Committee or Guardians shall be appointed in like manner as the first, and so on from year to year as long as the said Association shall exist.

III.

That the Members of each Colliery shall appoint one from amongst their Members who shall be deemed a Sub-Committee man, and that such Sub-Committee man, so to be appointed as aforesaid, shall appoint from amongst them three persons, who shall be Stewards of the said Society : and that all such Sub-Committee shall meet every fortnight, at the office of the said Society in Newcastle, in order to transact the business of the said Society ; and that the Stewards shall also attend, with the Clerk, in order to receive the contributions : which said Sub-Committee shall be removed after being in such capacity for twelve months ; and that the new Sub-Committee shall from time to time be appointed in the like manner as the first Sub-Committee, which said Sub-Committee shall have an executive power ; and that the said Stewards shall remain in office for twelve months, and their successors appointed in the like manner as those first appointed.

IV.

That no Member who shall belong to the General Committee or Guardians, Sub-committee, Stewards, or any person filling any situation in this Society, shall remain in any of the capacities aforesaid, or shall have a vote in the appointment of such General Committee or Guardians, Sub-committee or Stewards, after such person or persons shall have ceased being Coal Hewers, or who shall not have acted in that capacity for the last six months. And immediately upon any person or persons so ceasing to be a Hewer as aforesaid, in every such case a new appointment or appointments shall be made in the like manner as is provided for the original appointment : but that, before any such appointments can be complete, the person or persons so appointed shall produce a certificate, signed and properly attested by the Committee-man of the Colliery from whence such appointment shall have arisen, that such person is a Coal Hewer, and has acted in that capacity for the last twelve months : and without such certificate no such appointment shall be valid or of any avail.

V.

That no Member or Members shall remain longer, either as one of the General Committee or Guardians, Sub-committee, or in any other situation, after such person or persons shall have been declared, by a majority of the said General Committee or Guardians, to have acted improperly ; and such person or persons from thenceforth shall cease being in any of the capacities aforesaid, or be able to act in such situation for two years ; and that immediately after every vacancy, arising as aforesaid, a new appointment or appointments shall be forthwith made in the same manner as the first appointment.

VI.

That no Member of this Society shall earn more than four shillings and sixpence per diem, while employed under ground in the Coal Mines, for each day and every day. Nor shall any such Member or Members work in the Mines as hewers, shift work, or what may be deemed equal to shift work, above eight hours in every twenty-four hours: nor any such Member or Members, being hired by the day, shall not work under ground above twelve hours in every twenty-four hours, being taken for the whole six days in the week. And in case any such Member or Members being a hewer, earning above four shillings and sixpence per day, shall forfeit not only the said four shillings and sixpence, but all such other sum or sums of money as he shall so earn over and above the said four shillings and sixpence. And any Member or Members working double shifts, or a shift and a half, or twelve hours within twenty-four hours, he or they being hewers and shifters, shall be fined five shillings over and above the said four shillings and sixpence so to be earned as aforesaid. And in case any Member or Members shall not well and truly state to the proper Officers of this Society the amount of his earnings; or shall either directly or indirectly defraud, or attempt to defraud, the Society of his or their said earnings, or fines, or forfeitures, in any or either of the said cases, such Member or Members shall forfeit double the sum such Member or Members shall have so kept back, or defrauded, or attempted to defraud as aforesaid. And any Member or Members working above eight hours and twelve hours as aforesaid, shall forfeit sixpence for every hour he or they shall work over and above the said eight hours and twelve hours. All the before mentioned forfeitures to be paid to the general Fund of the said Society.

VII.

That each and every Member of this Society leaving their respective Colliery, and going to another Colliery, shall have a certificate from the Clerk or Stewards, certifying such Member or Members has or have paid all their Contributions; and such Member or Members shall not be deemed an efficient

Member or Members until he has produced to the Committee-man, belonging such new employment, such certificate; which such Committee-man is required to indorse the date when the same is received, and return such certificate at the next Monthly Meeting, to be filed with the papers belonging the said Society : and no benefit or advantage to be derived therefrom until proof is given that such certificate has been duly and faithfully obtained and delivered to the Committee-man belonging the new employment.

VIII.

That each and every Member of this Society shall well and faithfully pay fourpence halfpenny weekly and every week, on the expiration of every fortnight, to the respective Stewards or the Committee men of the said Society; who are required to enter the several payments in books to be kept for that purpose ; and at the next fortnight meeting, the same to be paid over to the proper officer, and by him entered in a general book ; and such sums of money shall be placed to the general fund of the said Society, to be applied to the purposes of the same : and immediately upon the funds amounting to one hundred pounds, and not required to be applied immediately to the Society, the same to be invested in government securities, in the names of five of the General Committee or Guardians of the said Society.

IX.

That all the officers and other persons intrusted with the funds of the said Society, shall give security for the due administration of the same, by warrant

of attorney, in order the more effectually to protect
the money belonging this Society: and in case any
of the persons last mentioned shall refuse to have his
or their accounts examined, or shall act in any manner improperly, and being found, by a majority of
the General Committee or Guardians, to have so
conducted themselves, shall be fined, for every such
offence one guinea, and shall not receive any benefit
from this Society for one year.

X.

That any Member or Members of this Society,
from lameness, or from ill health, not being able to
work under ground, or in the coal mines, and can
be employed above bank, shall still continue a Member or Members hereof, upon paying his or their respective proportions hereinbefore and hereinafter provided to be paid, and complying with all the Rules
and Bye Laws of the said Society; and such Member or Members shall work or employ himself or
themselves in such manner as he or they shall deem
proper.

XI.

That no person shall become a Member hereof
until he has paid a sum of money equal to what has
been paid by any one Member belonging the Colliery in which such person is employed who proposes
to become a Member, and also submitting to the
several Rules and Regulations of the said Society:
and all and every person or persons, being Colliers,
belonging to the rivers Tyne and Wear, shall be admitted until the twentieth day of February, one
thousand eight hundred and twenty-six, upon the

payments being made as last aforesaid, and on executing these presents. And from and after the twentieth day of February, one thousand eight hundred and twenty-six, no person shall be admitted to become a Member hereof, but upon paying an additional sum of five shillings over and above the payments aforesaid ; and from and after the twenty-eighth day of May, one thousand eight hundred and twenty-six, no person shall become a Member hereof, but upon paying an additional sum of ten shillings, and also the sum of money before mentioned, and shall not become a full Member until one whole year after such Member has so entered himself.— And that no person or persons shall be suffered to enter this Society under the age of eighteen years, or above sixty years of age ; nor shall any person, after the first day of January, 1829, become a Member hereof, who is above the age of forty-five years. And from and after the last mentioned period, all persons becoming Members, who shall not exceed the age of twenty-one years, shall, upon and before his so becoming a Member, pay the sum of ten shillings, and to be a free Member. And all persons becoming Members as last aforesaid, and not exceeding thirty years, shall, before becoming such Member, pay the sum of five pounds, and be three years before he is a free Member. Provided always, and it is the true intent and meaning of these presents, that all the persons last mentioned, becoming Members after the first day of January, 1829, shall be three years a Member hereof before such person or persons can become full Members hereof, and entitled to the

benefits and advantages of the said Society; but shall
be bound to make the contributions hereinbefore and
hereinafter mentioned, and be subject to the several
Rules and Regulations of the said Society.

XII.

That no Member of this Society shall bind himself
in any contract, in writing, without such contract has
been perused and approved of by the Solicitor for
this Society, in order thereby that all the Members
hereof may be fully aware of the effect of the contract he or they enters into. And no Member shall,
on any account, contract for working less than eleven
days in each fortnight, during the whole year;
namely, six days in one week and five days the other
week : nor shall such Members bind themselves to
work on the pay Saturdays. And further, that no
Member of this Society shall, on any pretence whatsoever, enter into any contract for service until twelve
hours after the expiration of his former contract.
And any Member not strictly complying with the
agreements last hereinbefore mentioned, or who shall
sign any contract not strictly conformable with the
last mentioned agreements, shall be immediately excluded from this Society, and be for ever rendered
unable to become a Member hereof, or entitled to
any benefit or advantage from the same.

XIII.

That before any Member or Members hereof shall
become bound to any Colliery on the Tyne or Wear,
all the General Committee, Sub-Committee, Officers,
and others holding situations in this Society, shall
become bound in the first place, and in preference

to any of the other Members : and any Member offending against this Rule shall be immediately fined
one guinea, and receive no benefit for one year, for
the first offence ; and for the second offence, be excluded from all benefit arising from this Society.—
And that no Member shall bind himself to put with
trams, or act as barrow-man, set on corves, or do
the business of a driver or on-setter, banks-man, or
skreener, or any other work above bank whatsoever :
and any person so offending shall, for every such offence, forfeit to the funds of this Society, 10s. 6d.

XIV.

That every Member who shall, by sickness, ill
health, or through any accident, or blindness, or any
other infirmity whatsoever, be deprived of gaining
his or their livelihoods, he or they shall receive for
and during the first twenty-six weeks, the sum of
five shillings per week, weekly and every week ; and
from and after that period, the weekly sum of two
shillings and sixpence per week, for twenty-six
weeks ; and afterwards one shilling and threepence
per week, during the illness of such Member or
Members. But no sick-money to be allowed before
the 5th. of April, 1826. And upon the death of any
Member or Members, the sum of four pounds shall
be paid towards the funeral of each of such Member
or Members. And to the widow of each and every
Member, towards her funeral, shall be paid two
pounds ten shillings ; such widow's conduct, during
her widowhood, being approved of by the majority
of the General Committee or Guardians. And for
the funeral of every Member's child, born in lawful

wedlock, under fourteen years of age, the sum of one
pound ten shillings shall be paid towards such funeral. Provided always, and it is the true intent
and meaning of these presents, that no Member of
this Society shall receive any benefit from the same
until he shall have paid the sum of 19s. 6d. to the said
Society, exclusive of all fines. And that no legacy
shall be paid before the fifth of April, 1827.

XV

That any Member of this Society using any means
whereby to defraud the said Society, or not complying with all the Rules and Regulations of the same,
or obtaining sick-money while able to work, or becoming a habitual drunkard, or fighting, or contract-
ing the venereal disease, or being notoriously im-
moral, or speaking against the king or his government, after having notice thereof, shall be fined or
excluded, at the discretion of the General Committee
or Guardians.

XVI.

That no Member shall, while sick, be entitled to
receive any relief until he has given notice thereof
to the Committee-man of the Colliery where he belongs, accompanied with a surgeon's certificate, specifying such illness. And if such notice is given on
Saturday, Sunday, or Monday, such Member being
duly entitled to relief, shall be paid the same on the
Saturday following : but if such notice is not given
until after the Monday, then no relief shall be granted until the second Saturday after notice. And no
Member shall do any work whatever, either for
wages or otherwise, without the consent of the Com-

mittee-man belonging the Colliery where such sick Member had been employed ; and such Committee-man is required to forward, on the next monthly meeting of the General Committee or Guardians, what leave has been given to such sick Member to work, and the ground upon which the same was granted, in order that the Clerk to the Society may regularly enter the same in a book to be kept for that purpose.

XVII.

That all the Rules, Regulations, and Bye Laws, made and entered into by the General Committee or Guardians, and sanctioned and approved of by a general meeting, called for the special purpose, shall be as binding and conclusive upon all the members hereof, as if the same were or was component parts or part of these Rules. Such Rules, Regulations, and Bye Laws to be entered in a book to be kept for that purpose, and signed by the Clerk and all the General Committee or Guardians. And every new Rule, Regulation, and Bye Law shall be copied and posted up in the room where the General and Sub-Committee meetings shall be held, during three several meetings ; in order that all the members may be fully aware what has been entered into by the members hereof.

XVIII.

That any five members of this Society, having complied with all the Rules and Regulations, and paid their respective contributions, upon signing a requisition, stating the object they have in view to the Clerk of the Society, may call a General Meeting

of all the members hereof; either for the purpose of
rescinding any of the Rules and Regulations herein-
beforé made, or altering or amending the same, or
any other of the Rules and Regulations hereinafter
to be made, or any other of the Rules and Bye Laws
to be made in conformity with these Articles.

XIX.

That all fines and forfeitures shall go to the general Fund of the said Society.

XX.

That this Society shall not be dissolved, unless by
the sanction of five-sixths of the members; and any
member proposing its dissolution shall be immediately expelled.

XXI.

That if any member strike at another member, he
shall, for every such offence, forfeit two shillings and
sixpence : and if the member so struck at return the
blow, he shall also be fined two shillings and sixpence.   That if any of the General Committee or
Guardians, Sub Committee, Clerks, or other officers,
shall appear intoxicated while upon the business of
the Association, he or they respectively shall, for
every such offence, be fined 2s 6d.

XXII.

That each and every Colliery shall chuse and elect
twenty one members, to form a Sub Committee; from
which two Stewards shall be chosen, every month,
to act together with the Clerk, and do all and every
thing, in that Colliery, which is requisite and necessary for the good of this Society.   The Clerk and
one of the Stewards from each Colliery to attend the

monthly meetings of the General Committee in Newcastle regularly every month. That if any of the
Committee neglect attending the several meetings
hereinbefore appointed for that purpose, unless prevented by illness or other unavoidable impediment,
shall be fined, for each non-attendance, sixpence.—
That if the Stewards, or either of them, neglect attending to pay the sick money, he or they so neglecting shall be respectively fined, for each and every
such neglect, one shilling. And if any member use
any abusive language to the owners of the Collieries
to which he may belong, or their agents, or do not be-
have himself in a becoming manner to his superiors,
such member shall be fined, for every such offence, 5s.

XXIII.

That a Box, containing three keys, shall be provided for the use of this Society; in which shall be
deposited all monies, vouchers for money, and securities. books, papers, and other documents connected
with the said society or belonging the eto; and that
each of the said Stewards be entrusted with one of
the said keys : and that on no pretence shall the box
be opened, but in the presence of all the Stewards.
And that the Landlord of the house in which the said
box shall be deposited, shall give security, to the satisfaction of the General Committee or Guardians,
for the safe custody of the same, and the money, securities for money, and other papers and documents
placed therein.

FINIS.

J. Marshall,
Printer, Newcastle.

A

VOICE FROM THE COAL MINES;

OR, A

Plain Statement

OF THE

VARIOUS GRIEVANCES OF THE PITMEN

OF THE

TYNE AND WEAR:

ADDRESSED TO THE COAL OWNERS—THEIR HEAD AGENTS—

AND A SYMPATHIZING PUBLIC,

BY THE

COLLIERS

OF THE

UNITED ASSOCIATION,

OF

Durham and Northumberland.

South Shields:

PRINTED BY J. CLARK, JUN., MARKET PLACE.

1825.

A VOICE &c.

" WHATSOEVER YE WOULD THAT MEN SHOULD DO UNTO
YOU, DO EVEN SO TO THEM.—*JESUS CHRIST.*"

THIS sublime axiom of christian philosophy
which we have selected as our motto, affords a
correct and beautiful standard of moral right:
which ought to direct all men in their conduct
towards each other. As a leading doctrine of
the great Redeemer of man, it commands the un-
divided attention of every believer in the christian
revelation : in as much as it includes within itself
every social doctrine and duty, of our holy religion and common faith. In proportion as this
benevolent doctrine is received and acted upon
by mankind, will vice, oppression, extortion, and
every evil be diminished ; till finally they are
banished to the doleful regions from whence they
came, no more to harrass, disturb, and depopu-
late the world. It is however to be regretted
that so little attention is paid to this excellent
precept ; and that the mistaken selfishness of
our nature, sets itself in opposition against the
operation of what, would be highly conducive to
our own interests. This remark is fully verified,
in the oppressive conduct of our masters towards
us their servants, as we hope will be clearly seen
in the progress of these pages ; which it is our
anxious wish may arouse the sympathies of the
public, and touch the feelings of our masters.

Individual cases of misery are numerous, and when we behold them we feel some small compassion, and occasionally afford some small relief; and then the remembrance of them fades from our memory, to be thought of no more. But when the sufferings of a whole community are presented to our view—when we see old age and youth, children and delicate females, all involved in one common desolation, it is then that the kindlier feelings of our nature predominate, and we too feel what misery truly is. Such a picture of desolation and calamity, does the pitmen of the Tyne and Wear, present to their *masters* and the public, through the medium of this address.

The pitman labouring in the subterraneous cavern often 200 yards below the surface of the earth, and shut out from the cheering light of heaven the greatest part of his earthly existence, is at any time, and under the most favourable circumstances, an object of sympathy and commiseration. " It is a pleasant thing to behold the light," said Solomon, and he was right, for what is existence worth, when that privilege is denied us which is the greatest enjoyment of life. This however, is the existence of the pitman, who between labour and sleep, scarcely ever beholds the light of day. But this is not the only evil that his situation entails upon him, when he takes leave of his family to descend the pit, he knows not that he ever may behold them more. The dangers to which he is exposed are numerous and of a hidden description—the falling stone—the rush of waters—and the fiery explosion, are the tremendous odds, staked every day against his existence ; to no set of men do the beautiful words of our burial service apply with more force and propriety, than to the pitmen; "*in the midst of life we are in death.*" If however under all

these disadvantages, evils and dangers, the pitman obtained the means to make his home comfortable, and of diffusing a moderate plenty
around his humble table, he would never mur-
mer; he would under all his personal dangers be
cheerful and happy; but when after all his toils
and privations, he finds himself starving in a land
of plenty, his wife and his children destitute of
those things which his affection would gladly supply them with, but, which his earnings will by no
means allow, he then deems it high time to speak
out, in language that may be *heard* by his oppressors, and by all. On whatever side the pitman looks, he sees nothing but horror, darkness,
and oppression—*scripture—reason—humanity*, all
violated in his person. The word of God, which
recommends a spirit of universal charity; to even
the brute part of the creation, is overlooked with
regard to him: the solemn precept, "wrong not
the hireling of his wages" is as a dead letter to
his callous employers. *Reason* too, the gift of
God to man, by which he is raised above every
known being in the scale of existence, is outraged,
monstrously outraged, in our case. *Reason* does
not sanction the performance of an illiberal un-
feeling action. *Reason* does not prescribe to the
wealthy, the crime of grinding the face of the
poor labourer, who produces all that contributes
to their ease, comfort, and luxury. *Reason* does
not suggest the necessity of stinting the operative
labourer to scanty wages, to a wretched pittance
that will barely maintain existence, and keep body
and soul together. *Reason* does not impose impossible conditions upon the workman; conditions
that render the utmost efforts of his skill unavailing and useless. *Reason* does not teach that the
poor and humble classes of society, are beings
of an inferior nature, destitute of the passions,
tastes, desires, and feelings that belong to the
common nature of man.

It teaches us that all mankind are members of the same family, made out of the same material, animated by the same spirit, having the same passions and desires, the same hopes and fears. It declares that an unjust action is criminal and degrading to man. It recommends kindness and forbearance towards those, whom providence has placed under our care. It forbids, peremptorily forbids, the doing an unjust action, to the meanest child of the family of man. When we compare this view of what reason forbids, and what it commands, with the treatment which for years we have met with, we are obliged to say, reason in our case has been *outraged, monstrously outraged!*

When we reflect that man is a creature of feeling, we are astonished that humanity has been so far from the breasts of our masters, or their agents, as to prevent them from ameliorating our condition. We should have thought that the very selfishness of human nature would have interposed in our behalf, for how can a man be comfortable in his mind, when he is aware that all his pleasures and honours, are the product of an *infamous system*, pursued towards his workmen. All the best feelings of nature must be extinguished, before a man can be happy under such circumstances; for however far a man may deviate from the maxims of prudence and virtue; however far he may be hurried by the impetuosity of his passions, from the path of rectitude; however indifferent he may be to the painful results of his conduct, in reference to himself, he *is*, and *will* be affected by the pain his irregularities give to others. This is the soul-working sympathy of nature; and at such moments as these, the soul bursts forth from the fetters that chain it to sense; and when all the emotions of fellow feeling, benevolence, and generosity, predominate in the human breast. O! that in a moment like this, our masters would consider our situation, and amend our condition. Were they for a short time to change conditions with us, they would then fully understand, what the *oppressions, insults,* and *injuries* are of which we complain. How miserable would they be, with the slender comforts of a collier's cottage: existence would then be intolerable, and happiness would only live in name. O! that the voice of RELIGION, REASON, and HUMANITY, (the sacred things, in the name of which we plead,) might be heard and obeyed in our behalf. Need we put our masters in mind of our patience and forbearance, for years, that we have been suffering, many of the evils of which we are now complaining: while mechanics of all descriptions, have been forming *unions,* bettering their condition and improving their wages; we have remained the same. While the bread-loaf, butcher's meat and every other commodity, has been enhanced in value; we have remained silent, and put up (till we can do so no longer) with our privations.

An honourable member of the legislature,* himself a coal owner, has in his place, in the House of Commons, borne ample testimony to our *quiet demeanour,* our *invincible patience,* and *love of peace.* Neither is it our desire to to forfeit the excellent character, that the enlightened and humane member for Newcastle, has given us; by any *forcible* attempts, to better our condition. We deprecate the idea of a "stick," nor shall we resort to it, till we have tried every other method and exhausted every other means. We do not wish to use the language of dictation to our employers; we do not wish to employ threats of any description; we do not wish to be unreasonable in our demands; above all we wish

---

* Sir Matthew White Ridley, Bart.

to avoid uproar and confusion. We wish our condition to be mended by our masters themselves. We wish them to have the *glory* of taking up the cause of the oppressed workmen, and relieving them from the intolerable burdens under which they *heavily groan* That these oppressions and burdens may be removed, they beg leave most respectfully to submit a statement of them to your attention, as they have been handed from the different collieries, as follows.

STATEMENTS OF GRIEVANCES.

Number 1.

1. The low price for working the coal ; having only for round Coal 5s. 9d. ; for small 2s. 9d. per score, and for broken coal—round 5s. 3d, and small 2s. 6d.

2. The setting out or taking the coal from us when a little short of the measure at bank, when it is known that the corf has to come on the rollies above a mile, subject to several lifts, and accidents: the measure should be taken at the bottom.

3. Non-payment for " band stone" under 4 inches which is a great hardship.

4. The " laying out," or fining us 6d. when a 20 peck corf has 2 quarts of small stones in it, when it is often impossible to distinguish small stones or slates from coal, so feeble is the light emitted from the " Davy lamp" whereas was the pit better ventilated, candles might be used, and this evil partially remedied, though with candles this " laying out" would be an evil.

5. Fines " for bad separation" or too great a quantity of small coals, with the round : here the want of light, the lifts, the distance the corf has to travel, and the tenderness of the coals, militate

against the most skilful and conscientious workman. The corf should be examined in the pit.

6. When working coal the cross way, we are
not allowed to use powder for blasting ; which
makes the labour one third more; and for this we
are allowed nothing extra. Whereas if we had
better ventilation, powder might be used.

7. The fine of 2s. 6d. if we should be one day
off work, on our own account : and the having nothing, when our masters choose to lay us idle.

8. The general bad state of the pit for want
of a good circulation of air, by which our health
is affected, and often our lives endangered.

II.

1. Having no additional pay for "headways."
or working the cross way of the coal, which requires much more labour, and which was formerly
considered a fit thing for extra pay.

2. The fine of sixpence for any deficiency in
separating, the inferior, or rusty coal, from the
superior: whereas, the "safety lamp" emits so dim
a light, that it is utterly impossible in many cases,
to effect the complete separation required.

3. The enormous fine of 2s. 6d. for *one gill* of
small coal, found in the corf, in the pit; and the
extra fine of 1s. at the mouth of the pit, for the
same corf: contrary to the bond.

4. The large size of the measures, lately introduced, which compels the workmen to perform
more labour, than that, for which he is paid,
which is a *shameful imposition*, and an *intolerable
grievance*

III.

1. The general state of the pit as it regards the
air, which in consequence of bad ventilation is ex-
tremely pernicious to the health of the workmen,
in the middle of August 1825 the Thermometer

stood at 130 degrees, and had been so with little variation for six months before that period, in consequence of which one young man entirely lost his health, others have been much indisposed, and several have been off work for different periods. An allowance of six-pence per day is made to men who work in this *fiery furnace*, but for every hour they are short of the stipulated time a fine of two pence is levied upon them; the fact is, they must either work here, and lose their *health*, or have no employment at all and *starve*— Have the advocates for the abolition of Negro Slavery no time to turn their attention to the domestic slavery of those who are called "free born Britons."

2. The fine of one shilling for "Bad Separation" or having too many small coals in the corf; is certainly unjust: when it is considered, that in many instances such is the *tender* state of the coal, owing to the "Creep or thrust," that a piece of coal 4 lbs. weight is rarely to be met with; and when found will very readily break to pieces and especially when we consider the deficiency of the "tram way" which is so encumbered with props, that the corf in its progress towards the shaft, often comes with great force against them, producing a concussion, *which breaks the coals*—the " rolly way" is much the same, and the corf is sometimes *overturned*, which naturally injures the coals; nor is the corf free from accidents in the pit shaft; for by its pendulous motion it frequently comes in contact with the sides of the Shaft, and every blow that it receives after leaving the workman at the "Board" or place of working, till it arrives at Bank has a tendency to break the coal smaller. And for all these contingencies, the poor pitman is to be accountable, and if the corf does not please he must be fined one shilling: when perhaps he has not wrought for two shillings.

3. The " setting out" the corf which the *pitman loses*, for a difficiency of one quart out of 360, or a 20 peck corf containing 18 quarts to the peck: when it is notorious to any school boy, that the peck only contains 8 quarts dry measure, and that the coal peck (if double) should contain but 16 quarts. This is a great hardship upon the Pitman; when (as has been shown above) the many casualities the corf has to encounter on the " Tram and Rolly ways" and in the " Shaft," are taken into consideration; and particularly the extra measure; which might very well satisfy our Masters for any accidental shortness of measure, as every corf the pitman sends to bank as a twenty peck corf, contains in reality $22\frac{1}{2}$ pecks, or 40 quarts of coal, more per corf, than what he agreed to send, or is paid for; so that if a man were to send 16 full measure corves to bank per day he would receive 4s. and if he did this six days per week would make 24s. as the measure now is, but if the measure was honest, he would receive 4s. 6d. per day, or 27s. per week, so much difference do these 18 quart pecks make, both in the colliers labour and remuneration.

How galling is the consideration that though we are bound to send 20 pecks in our corf to bank, yet when we know that our corf contains 22 pecks and 7 quarts, but for want of the other quart it is taken from us, *and thus we labour in vain!*

4. The want of a proper tribunal for redress, where injuries are sustained by the workmen, in there work, is another great grievance.

However much a pitman may be *insulted, fined,* or *evil treated* by any petty officer he can gain nothing by complaining, he will be told from the highest to the lowest agent, that he is telling a falsehood, or, he may leave at the binding if he does not like his employ, on the other hand the *overmen, deputies,* and *kekers,* are encouraged, (and in some cases compelled) to bear hard upon the men.

5. The scarcity of work is another grievance, according to the bond between us and our employers, they are bound to find us work, or pay us 2s. 6d. per day, after laying us three days idle: but on occasions of this kind, when the three days are expired, we are set to work for a day or two, and then laid three days idle again, when we would be very willing to work : or when this is not the case, the daily quantity of our work is diminished so that speaking generally, the average wages of men in this colliery, is little more than twenty-five shillings per fortnight, out of which miserable pittance. there are several drawbacks.

6. The " safety-lamp" is another great evil to us; although much good was expected to result to the pitmen from its discovery, and use in the collieries : the reverse however has been the case ; accidents have been nearly as frequent, and disasterous since, as before its introduction into the coal mines. But if we admit that it may occasionally prevent an explosion, and save us from premature death, yet on the other hand it is accessary to the destruction of our health ; bringing on rapid old age, and general imbecility. This is effected not directly, but indirectly by the " safety-lamp" which will be clearly seen by a reference to its introduction, and tracing its history. When the lamp was introduced proper allowance was made to the workmen for working with it, and no bad aired place was wrought in ; but when repeated experiments have proved what the lamp will do, the case is altered : now we have no allowance for the lamp, and the worst and most dangerous places can be wrought ; even when the steel mill might prove in some cases unsafe. Places are now at work, where the air is so inflamable, that the lamp is frequently red hot; and sometimes it is extinguished, and the danger to the workmen very great in consequence.

From this general use of the lamp, there results *a great saving* to the coal owners, (it being but a small part of the viewer's duty to consider the comfort, and health of the poor pitman,) as the pit can be carried on, without any particular, or expensive attention to the ventilation of the mine. It is evident to any man, the least acquainted with pit-work, that where the mine is the most dangerous, air might be forced, so as to render it perfectly safe, to work even with candles.

IV.

1. Limitation of work—We are only allowed to work nine days a fortnight, this may meet the views, and answer the purposes of our masters, but it certainly does little for us : we are willing to work, and desirous to work, that we may support ourselves and families and yet our work is withheld from us —This system is highly unreasonable, as it entails much misery upon the workmen without any just cause, if employment could not be found for the men why were they bound ! And how easy might the present work be equalized, if the interests of the men were considered, instead of sometimes doing nothing, and then again working at extremity

2. " The laying out" the corf for slates or stones being found in it ; and fining us sixpence for the same, when it often is no fault of ours.

3. Helping up the " barrowmen or putters," is another grievance that is worthy of complaint ; for if a man accomplish his days work in 8 hours, he has still to remain, till all the coals he has excavated, are taken off to be drawn to bank, thus prolonging his time to ten, twelve, or fourteen hours, in an *unhealthy* and *dangerous* place.

4. The small wages that we make is another evil ; while working men in general are making from twenty to thirty shillings per week, the

pitman here are only making thirteen shillings and sixpence, and from this miserable pittance the following deductions are made, $7\frac{1}{2}$d. for candles the caller and smith 1d. 3d. for house rent and fire, at least 3d. for picks and pick handles, making 1s. $2\frac{1}{2}$d. per week, and if we add 1s. for fines and forfeits will make 2s. $2\frac{1}{2}$d. leaving only 11s. $3\frac{1}{2}$d. for *our week's wages.* It is surely time for us to lift up our voice, and let our case be made known; human nature cannot endure *privations like these;* to be silent would be *criminal;* not to make an effort to shake of our chains, would prove that we *deserved* to *wear* them, and that we ought to sink under them.

V.

It would be almost impossible, and might appear frivolous, to enumerate all the grievances that we as workmen, labour under in this colliery: we shall only confine ourselves to a few, and state them with the greatest plainness, and,

1. Our bond is too rigorous, and contains conditions which it is impossible for us to comply with. The bond makes it imperative upon us to send "to bank," round or large coal, at 4s. 8d. per score, and small at 2s. 0d. per score: but if the round coal should be mixed with small coal, then the poor unfortunate workman is fined 1s. 0d.; or rather if the corf should be deemed so mixed, by the keker,* whose mere *assertion,* is quite sufficient for the purpose. Now this fine is both *absurd* and *oppressive,* for no line of distinction is drawn between round and small; what the workmen may deem a good corf, the keker's caprice may make a bad one. There is also a strong bias towards self interest in this

---

* A petty contemptible officer, appointed by the masters to watch the men's work and fine them.

petty spy, if he does not fine the men, and show some work for his wages, he must walk about his business; he knows that his masters will not pay him wages for nothing; therefore he labours *diligently* in his *disgraceful calling*, to the great oppression of his fellow men. Besides he may have a private pique at some men, and by fining them, he "kills two birds with one stone," or in other words, pleases his masters and gratifies his own bad passions. We can number of these petty officious understrappers, no less a number than eleven, upon our colliery. But our fine. system does not end here; if 2 quarts of splints or stones are found in a corf we are fined six-pence, and if more than that quantity is found we are *mercifully* fined the trifling and very moderate sum of *five shillings!!!* And should a corf want one quart of measure, that corf is forfeited to the owner. We certainly (if we had any thing like fair-play) ought when a corf is short of measure, to have pay for what is really produced by our labour: and when stones are accidentally found in a corf (for no man will put them in on purpose,) the workman ought to have the privilege of picking them out, and at any rate not be fined till he refuses to do so, which no man would when his own interest was so intimately concerned.

It ought to be observed here, that all the coals that fall off the corves, and which contribute to make what the "keker" calls short measure, are carefully gathered up for the engine fires, and general use of the colliery. Upon the whole it is evident, that eleven "kekers" would not be employed and encouraged, if the master did not find an interest in it, and more than an equivalent to the wages paid them, in consequence of this system, and other unavoidable expenses, it is no uncommon thing for the pitman, to have from 5 to 8 shillings per fortnight taken off his wages; which leaves a paltry sum no way adequate to supply the bare necessaries of his family, we might be asked here, why we thus bind ourselves, to such rigorous conditions; to this we might give many answers, the time which is selected by our masters for the entering upon this engagement is when the demand for our labour is in small request, and when in fact, we are almost compelled to accept of any terms. And we are further induced to bind ourselves, under these degrading and oppressive conditions, from the hope we indulge from time to time, that our masters will begin to see the propriety of treating us in a more liberal manner. And lastly from our repugnance to any thing like a " strike" for wages or privileges : and the patience with which the pitmen have borne their accumulated burdens, for the last ten years, proves the truth of our assertion.

The bad ventilation of the mine is another great grievance under which we labour, to save expense our health and our lives, are almost continually endangered.

Sir Humphrey Davy's invention of the safety lamp has been an advantage to the coal owners ; but a great injury to the comfort and earnings of the pitmen : for while the former may remain indifferent about the safety of the mine, and neglect to form the proper supply of atmospheric air to the inner parts of the pit, on account of the great power of the lamp to resist combustion or explosion; the poor miner has to suffer the most awful agony in an exceedingly high temperature, inimical to his *health, comfort,* and even *life.* Instances could be given by us if needful, to prove the truth of what we have just stated ; and every man on the colliery, will bear testimony to the fact.

The manner in which our masters evade the terms of the bond, is another great grievance, the bond expresses an obligation on the side of the masters to pay us 2s. 6d. per day, if we are laid idle more than three days, on their account; and Mr Buddle in his examination before the " select committee on combination laws." roundly asserts that our " employers engage to give us 2s. 6d. per day whether we are employed or not;" and he goes further then even this, his words, (as copied from the minutes of evidence,) are, " If we" (meaning the coal owners) " cannot sell coals to give them full employment, *we are not to give them less than 2s. 6d. per day*"—Now if a working collier had stepped immediately into this " Engineer's" place, and one of the honorable members had asked these questions.

Does it frequently happen, that you have not " full employment"—the answer would be,

Collier. Yes nine months out of the twelve for which we are bound.

Member—Then I suppose from what Mr. Buddle has just stated, if you should work for less than £1. 10s. in the fortnight, your owners will make up the deficiency to you.

Collier. Nothing of the kind—

Member. Come recollect yourself; can you remember no instance of your wages coming only to 25 shillings in the fortnight, and of your masters or their agents, making you a present of 5 shillings to make up the deficiency.

Collier. I believe I have as good a memory as any man; and I can well remember the wages being frequently 25 shillings per fortnight, and even less.

Member. Well then the kindness of your masters in making them up to 30 shillings, has not been forgotten I hope.

Collier. Indeed Sir, it is bad remembering what never took place.

Member. Do you mean to say that Mr. Buddle, has been deceiving this honorable committee?

Collier. Indeed I do Sir, the facts of the case are simply these. There is a clause in the bond to the effect of what Mr. Buddle has mentioned,

B

which binds, or ought to bind, our masters to make up our wages: but this very clause has a qualifying clause connected with it, which completely throws all the power into their own hands, so that by a little skilful manœuvring, the bond, without legally breaking it, is *evaded to the injury of the men.*

Member. You confound me, would your masters degrade themselves by any kind of low trickery, to wrong you out of your wages? What do you mean, explain yourself.

Collier. That, Sir, I can readily do. I am inclined to think that our masters would not do so, but that their agents do so, is a notorious fact. In the clause that I referred to in the bond, the owners only engage to pay us 2s. 6d, for such day or days as we are by them laid idle; but not till after the lapse of three days: and what I alluded to by "skilful manœuvring" is this, on any slack of work, they will lay the pit in three days, and on the fourth day they will work, and then if they please lay the pit in three days more, without paying us a farthing; and which according to the "clause" we cannot compel them to do; as they stick to the letter of the bond, instead of the spirit. If you think, Sir, that I have stated any thing wrong, call Mr. Buddle in again, I dare say that little man in the corner has written down all I have said; and he will have the goodness to read it over to him, and let him on his oath contradict me if he can. This would have been something like a true representation of the case; a representation, which Mr. Buddle *could not have denied, without perjuring himself.*

Now, we would put it to any reasonable man, whether the way in which we are treated, is either honorable or just: setting aside the large measure of 18 quarts to the peck, by which our work is measured; is not every part of the conduct of our masters marked by *inhumanity, oppression,* and *injustice* toward us. Can human nature endure such a continued series of injury without complaining, and *endeavouring to shake off the yoke of bondage.*

VI.

1. *An unreasonable and oppressive Bond.*—We work for money, but it is at the pleasure of our masters to take it from us, we, not having the power to claim one farthing, if they chuse to construe the bond, in the most rigid sense: in point of fact they can go (what appears almost inconceivable,) even further than this; they can make *us pay for doing the work for them!!* We need only refer to the bond, to prove this assertion; which says, "If a corf of coals should have a quart of foul coals, splint or stone in it, we are to forfeit 3d; and if a corf has to the amount of two quarts, 6d; and for three quarts, 9d; or be deemed guilty of a misdemeanor, and be fined 5s; or confined in the House of Correction." It is true, this utmost rigour of the bond is not resorted to, yet it is held in terrorem over the head of the poor collier, and he knows not how soon he may become the victim of the shameful contract he is compelled to sign.

2. The fine of 1s. for small coals being mixed with the large coals, is another intolerable grievance. It is well known that coal is of a very brittle nature, and when it is considered that the coal has many accidents to meet with, in its progress from that part of the mine where it is excavated, to the mouth of the pit; it is exceedingly hard, that we should be fined for a thing over which we have no controul. And then, we have no one to stand up and plead for us; the keker being an officer appointed by our masters, is to us what Pharoah's task masters were to the Israelites: "making us serve with rigour." And

many instances occur of the poor and industrious collier having 1s. 6d. or 2s. taking from him in a day; by the unjust exertion of despotic power. And should any resistance be made to this *detestable tyranny*, and a magistrate be applied to, the influence of the agent, together with the bond, is sure to cast the pitman, if his cause be ever so just. The following statement will convey a very moderate view of what is taken from a working collier's small wages, every fortnight.*

	s.	d.
For "set out" and "laid out." . . .	1	10
For House-Rent, Fire, &c.	0	6
For repairing Work Tools	0	3
For Candles	1	0
For Gunpowder to blast the Coal . .	0	8
	4	3

Here we see, that with fines and other extras, nearly £6. a year is taken from our wages ; and this is a very moderate average. *Can human nature sustain such impositions?*

VII.

In this colliery, we are working, what is called, separation, having 7s. a score for round, and 2s. a score for small coal. For every corf that is deemed mixed, that is, having small coals in it, we have to forfeit 1s., whereas we are only paid about $4\frac{1}{4}$d for hewing it. Now this fine is unjust and unreasonable, because the coal is so tender, that it almost breaks of itself: it has two miles to travel underground ; the corf is continually shaking, and meeting with obstructions : and the keker appointed to inspect the corf, has very little knowledge of the matter, and generally

---

* We have sometimes more than double this sum in the fortnight, and some men have been fined 4s. in a day, and 2 men were once fined £1 in a fortnight.

without much hesitation exclaims, " *This corf is set out.*" This takes away the value of 3 corves from the workman, and leaves him little more than 1s. 6d. or 2s. for his day's work. And this is all done, without any person being appointed in behalf of the workman, to enquire into the matter. The mere "ipse dixit" of the keker, is quite sufficient to rob the poor collier of 1s. for which he has wrought hard. Every pains is taken to protect the interests of the masters, but the men are unprotected, and often *very fraudulently treated.*

2. The next imposition of which we complain, is the fine of 6d, levied upon us when one quart of stone is found in a corf. And when two quarts are found, it is deemed a misdemeanor, and the business is left to the agents, to fine us 5s. or 10s. at their discretion!! As there are small coals, for which we have only $1\frac{1}{4}$d a corf, we surely can be under no temptation to fill them up with stones.

3. The fine of 6d when any portion of rusty, or red coal is found in a corf, when it is nearly impossible to distinguish them, by the faint, bad light of the " Davy lamp."

4. Instead of the masters giving us encouragement for working the mine so far in ; which saves them the great expense of sinking a new shaft or pit, they make us suffer more and more.

Nothing can be conceived more detrimental to the health of the miner, than the air which he inhales in this situation : for the atmospheric air passing through a vast track of subterraneous space, carries with it, all the noxious vapour, and gaceous substances, which are accumulated in the mine : so that the pitman may be said to inspire DEATH, in every breath that he draws.

5. Another grievance is the removal of many of our privileges, formerly we had allowance made of so much per yard, in places of difficult

work : for candles and gunpowder : binding money, &c. &c. But these things have all been by little and little taken from us. The viewers evince great sagacity in the reduction of wages : they must have credit, for understanding the nature of Englishmen : they never lay on too great a burden at one time, but proceed by imperceptible degrees. When they want to effect a reduction, they say, " we intend to take of 3d. a score, or otherwise you must find your own candles." The men only have choice between two evils, and they choose the least—they find their own candles. Next year, when it is presumed, the men have forgotten that they had their candles found ; they proceed a little further, and take off the 3d. a score. And this is the way that one imposition after another, has been laid upon the collier, from year to year, till their grievances have arisen to the *frightful height* which are here detailed ; and which they can bear no longer. Between hope and despair they exclaim,

> Poor men suffer, good men grieve,
> Knaves devise, and fools believe ;
> Help, O Lord, send aid unto us,
> Or knaves, and fools, will quite undo us.

VIII.

1. We are bound to work six days a week, but our masters have reduced our labour to five days : and on these days we are obliged to work nearly 10 hours, for the paltry sum of 2s. 9d. ; which makes only 13s. 9d. per week. Will this sum keep a single man comfortable, and clothe him properly ? not without the exercise of the most rigid economy. What then must be the fate of a family, who are obliged to make this sum do.

2. The " set out" and " laid out," is another great grievance, which we labour under : our 13s. 9d. per week, is broken in upon, in the most

shameful manner. Persons who are strangers to the hardships of the colliers, will scarcely believe, that many hard working, honest men, have to sacrifice 2 and sometimes 3 shillings per week, by their arbitrary regulations, in reference to those corves, which are deemed by the keker, short measure, or have a small quantity of splinty coal, or stone in them. It was formerly the practice of this colliery, to allow the men to measure the stones, that happened to be in a corf; but now this is done away, and the corf is condemned, and the stones *thrown away, before the pitman ascends the mine;* so that the keker has the power to condemn a man's work, at his *sovereign pleasure,* without adducing any proof. And as it regards the measure, we have several times been at the master, to allow a proper measure tub, to be upon the colliery, which has been constantly refused : and we have strong suspicions, that the peck, by which the size of the corf is regulated, is 17 quarts, instead of 16, the legal measure.

IX.

1. We object to the fine of 1s , for what is called " bad separation," or the corf being mixed with small coals. No man will fill up his corf improperly, if he can possibly help it ; and we believe that in 19 cases out of 20, when men are fined for this thing, the deficiency, or improper mixture of the coals proceeds from accident, over which he has no controul ; and he might with as much propriety be fined a shilling every day that it *rains.* Let any reasonable master, (and we think we have such a master,) reflect for a moment how utterly impossible, in the majority of cases, when this fine is exacted, it is for the pitman to prevent it ; when a corf is filled at the " board" or place of excavation, with the greatest care by the workman, the tender nature of the coal, and the various

concussions it meets with in the way to the "bank"
or the top of the pit, has a great tendency to reduce the coal, and make a portion of them small.
How hard then it is, upon the poor miner, to be
accountable for all accidents that may happen to
spoil his work. And instances are common enough,
of two or three of these shilling corves, falling to
the lot of one man in a day.   Does Algiers or
Tunis with all their despotism, present to the
mind of the moral observer, any thing like this, in
the whole course of their *tyrannical annals?* In
fact, the evil calls loudly for removal, men *cannot*
bear it—it is as *disgraceful* to the parties who enforce it, as *degrading* to the men who submit to it.

2. There is another forfeit of one shilling, that
exceeds the former in imposition. In working the
large coal, we have the small coals to throw back ;
they are denominated by us, " dead small," for
this we get nothing, although we have them to
work.   But this does not end the history of the
" dead small;" they are wanted for engine fires,
or the workmen's houses, and then we have to fill
them up ; (observe gentle reader, for nothing,) and
if there should happen to be among this " dead
small," a few stones, we are fined *one shilling !!!*
It seems as if our agents could not *exist but in the
atmosphere of fines and forfeits.*

3. The forfeiting of the corf, when it is not
deemed measure by the keker, is another imposition which the men have to endure. With a corf
of 22 pecks, they insist that the men, are to take
their hands, and thrust in a piece of coal, wherever
there is a " hole or corner," and if his corf should
want, but a handful of being full, (according to
their ideas of filling,) he forfeits the whole !!! Now
is not this shameful ; why might not the man have
pay for what he has done ; supposing there was a
peck short of measure, why could not one farthing
suffice ? this would be more than the pitman gets

for his labour.—Is it not robbery, downright robbery, to take the whole from us?

4. The fine of 6d. for what we call "chennelly"
or half round and half small coal. When the
seam is soft and bad, and large coal cannot be
procured, then these are wrought: we have only
4s. 6d. per score for working them; and yet labour under this sixpenny fine, if the corf does
not suit, when brought to bank.

5. The working 8 days per fortnight, and at
stinted labour, is another great evil, that we have
to suffer; as a man has not the opportunity of
making his labour sufficiently productive, to meet
the wants of his family, and consequently has to
live in a *half starved condition*. And then, with
this conduct in our view, we, on the other hand,
are fined 2s. 6d. if we should, (however lawful
the cause,) absent ourselves a single day from our
labour, unless we produce a certificate from the
surgeon certifying we are ill. Now how shameful this is; the pitman may have private business
to attend to, as well as any other man, his family
may be at a distance, some of them may be ill,
a brother may wish to see him, and many other
things of a similar kind; but as if the loss of his
day's work was not sufficient for him to suffer,
2s. 6d. more must be added This we really believe never comes into the pocket of the owner,
nor do we believe that he knows any thing about it.

6. The compelling us to remain idle 14 days
at Christmas. which during that season, either
forces us to *starve*, or run into *debt*; and it often
happens to be near Christmas again, before it is
liquidated, and then we are soon in as bad a
plight as before.

7. The fine of 10s. 6d. for offending a boy, is
another shameful thing levied upon the pitman.
The boys who assist the men, are not easily kept
to their duty, as every one will know, who has

apprentices. But if a boy be ever so *unruly, impertinent*, or *lazy*, the man has to suffer for all. And as every man is not endued with an inexhaustable stock of patience, some may be so far irritated, as (to use our own phrase,) to take him a "clout;" but if the boy complains, the question is not put, What were you doing? the man is not enquired at, in order to ascertain how the matter *really stood;* but is, or may be, fined 10s. 6d. without any hesitation: now observe, this does not go to the boy, but goes into the pocket of the owners, or agents, probably the latter.

8. We complain of the insolent and contemptuous manner, in which we are generally treated by the agents, and men in office. We are absolutely treated, when we complain of any thing, as if we were devoid of all feeling as men, and fit only to herd with the common beasts of the field. When the poor man ascends the mine, and is informed, that so many of his corves are "set out" and "laid out," and finds that his day's work is reduced to nothing, under the feeling of the moment, he hurries to the office, either to remonstrate with the agents, or to beg of them to consider his *family*, and *situation*, and release him from the burden of these fines and forfeits; but instead of being received in a humane manner by the men who are his brothers, a number of *frivolous, ignorant*, and *impertinent* questions are put to him, in a most contemptuous manner Are you a union man?—What will your union do for you?—Dont you think you are all wrong?— Thus are the feelings of the poor fellow insulted and outraged, and all for no purpose.

If ever an association was formed upon just grounds, ours is that association; for never did the sun of heaven shine upon a more *degraded, oppressed* race of human beings than we are. Our agents *know this*, as well as we do ourselves.

And yet, gracious Heaven! they insult us with our union. O righteous God of heaven, give us patience, that we may conduct ourselves as we ought, till thou in the exercise of thy good providence undertake for us, and bless the legal means we are employing, to induce our masters to rectify this long catalogue of abuses under which we groan.

X.

1. We complain of the "set out" or the taking the corf from us, for being, what our masters, call short measure, that is, wanting 1 quart, when it is known that the corf has to be twice lifted, go over 400 *yards of incline plane*, and also the rolly way, and shaft; in all of which places, it is exposed to lose the coals off the top. And without once considering these things, the pitman is blamed, has his corf taken from him, and loses, of course, $3\frac{1}{2}$d. This is a serious loss to the miner, especially when 2, 3, or 4 corves are "set out" in a day, which sometimes happens. And it is worthy of observation, that they will not allow one man to help out another, if he were ever so willing !!

2. We complain of the "laid out." When we send a corf to bank, of the value of $1\frac{1}{2}$d, and 1 quart of stone is found in it, we are fined 6d, which is four times the value of the corf. And if the "seam" or strata of coal be of the foulest and worst description, still no lenity is shown to us, but the fine exacted in the most rigorous manner.

3. We complain of the fine of 2s. 6d. for splint being found in a corf. We have this splint to curve out of the middle of the seam, and it is almost impossible to keep clear of it at all times. In this fine, there is not the least proportion to the offence. In fact, it may be said, every time

the fine is exacted, we are robbed, unjustly robbed !!!

4. We complain of having no allowance for powder. Formerly we were allowed 1½lbs. per fortnight, but now we have to find the whole, which upon an average, amounts to 4lb. per fortnight, which has long cost us 2s. 8d., as we bought it of the agent; but now, when we buy it ourselves, it only costs us 2s. which is a saving of 17s. a year, or £80 to 100 men! But still we contend, that it is a great hardship, that our former allowance should be taken off us, or that we have any powder to buy at all, to do our master's work with.

5. We complain of being bound to 8 days per fortnight.

6. We complain of being laid idle 14 days at Christmas, which is a great drawback upon poor men, who can hardly live with constant work.

XI.

1. We are compelled to lead our own coals, which we believe, is not the case with any colliery in the North of England.

2. We complain of finding our own dwelling-houses : now in other collieries, the men have their houses found them ; for paying 6d. per fortnight. That we should be made to differ is exceedingly hard.

3. We complain that when we are sick, or have been lamed, they find no doctor : as is the usage of other coal works.

4. We complain of having no "smart money" or weekly allowance, made to us, when we have been lamed in following the work of our employer.

5. We find our own candles ; whereas they ought to find at least a part of them.

6. We complain of the very low score-price ; having only 3s. 4d. per score for round ; 2s. 4d.

for " chennelly" or half round ; and 10d. for small coal. Which puts it out of the power of any man to make any thing *like a living*. A man for instance, may have 30 corves in a day ; but 17 of them are small coal, for which we only receive one halfpenny each, which is 8½d. ; and the other 13 " chennelly," which comes to 1s 8d¼. making only 2s. 2d¾. for the whole days work !!! Listen O Heavens! and give Ear O Earth.

And it sometimes happens, that a man labours, 7 hours, for 9 of these small corves; or in other words for 4½d. !!!

7. We complain of the small price we have for working yard work ; which is only sixpence per yard : when it frequently happens, that after a man has exerted all his *strength* and *skill*, he can only cut one yard, and hew 12 corves, amounting to the horrible small sum of 1s. 10d½. for his days labour. And cases have occurred, where the coals have been all small, and then the poor collier's remuneration, for his day's work, has been only 11d. !!! And when we complain of such dreadful treatment, we are frowned upon, and called grumbling dissatisfied fellows. But then this is not all ; if 2 quarts of stone, be found in one of these corves, for which we receive only *one half-penny*, they will fine us sixpence! And if a corf should want 1½ pecks of being full, they will take it from us, when they *know* that the corf is 17½ pecks instead of 16, to which we are bound.

8. We complain of our master, frequently compelling us, to work 14 hours ; and when worn out with labour, if we should leave at the end of 10 hours, they *mercifully* fine us 2s. 6d. And if we should be one day idle (and a man may some times want a day's liberty,) they fine us 2s.

9. We complain of the improper manner we have to work. It sometimes occurs, that after we have been kept in the *doleful hole*, till 5 o'clock

in the evening, we are ordered back again at 12 at night; and kept 14 hours; and often half of that time, we are lying in the pit idle: under the pretence that the coal is not *just then wanted.* Thus we are kept from the light of heaven, and exposed for hours to the inflamable air, to the great injury of our *health,* and our *lives.* Surely if there existed the least particle of humanity, in the breasts of our masters, they would not sanction such a state of things as we in our complaints have referred to. One writer has well observed, " A generous master compassionates the lot of those, who are obliged to toil for his benefit or gratification. He lightens their burdens; treats them with kindness and affection; studies to promote their interest and happiness; and, as much as possible, conceals from *them, their* servitude, and *his* superiority. On the distinctions of rank and fortune, he does not set too high a value: and though the circumstances of life require, that there should be *hewers of wood,* (coal) *and drawers of water,* yet he forgets not, that mankind are by nature equal; all being the offspring of God, the subjects of his moral government, and joint heirs of immortality. A conduct like this, gives a master claims which no money can purchase; no labour can repay. His affection can only be compensated by *love;* his kindness by *gratitude;* and his cordiality, by the service of the *heart.*" How much, would the kind, simple, warm hearted collier, revere and love a master, who answered the above portrait. But alas! how different—like the laws of Draco, so are our laws, " *Written in Blood.*"

XII.

Our case is nearly similar, in the general features, to several other of the complaining collieries. The awful system of " laying out" and "setting out," fines and forfeits, exist with us in all their oppressive force. Our stated earnings are too small by almost one half: in fact it is matter of wonder, how men situated as we are, work any at all; the small pittance we receive, being scarcely adequate to support existence in its most *feeble state*. There are two grievances which seem to be peculiar to our colliery, which we shall mention. The first is, the small strata of brass, in the middle of the seam ; which breaks away with the coal, and in filling up the corf, should a small piece or two get in, (which will happen in the hand of the most careful man) we are fined 6d. or a 1s. or just what our masters please.

2. The Waggon drivers are compelled to remain at work fifteen hours, and then only receive 1s. 2d. this is a shameful thing ; outraging the feelings of every tender parent ; and injuring *deeply* injuring the health of the boys.

––––––––––

Having thus stated some of our grievances, it remains for the consideration of our masters, whether they will redress them or not. It must be palpable to our masters, that we have not given vent to our feelings, simply for the sake of complaining; or from whim, caprice, and mere turbulence ; we have " reasons, good and strong" for the step that we have taken, these reasons are exhibited, to our masters, and to the public, in the preceding pages, and there is not a collier in the district, who would not *stake his very existence* upon the truth of the statements made in this paper. We are fully aware, that many of the agents, will attempt to invalidate our public testimony, and represent us, as a set of grumbling, dissatisfied fellows ; never content with our work and wages : and that if we had our own way, we would take the whole profits of the collieries, from the masters, and still shew the same dissatisfaction of spirit. Let our masters take care how they listen, to the false representations of their agents ;

let them examine the matter impartially, or appoint jointly with the men, certain disinterested persons, to make a correct statement of the whole matter; this will be the way to come at the whole truth. It is utterly impossible, for men to be doomed to a more severe lot, than that which we endure. It is not against providence, that we disclaim,—that would be impious; we know that we must obtain our bread by labour; and that is all we desire : we hope for nothing better in this world : in fact it is the great end and aim, of all our efforts. But while we are oppressed in the manner we have described, we can have no hope to earn our bread, and obtain any thing like a comfortable living, for ourselves and families. We are cursed above the curse, which God pronounced upon Adam : he was doomed to sweat and labour; but we have *rags, poverty*, and *starvation*, added to our sweat and labour.

Besides this, from men arrayed, in a "little brief authority," and placed over us, we continually receive the most unmerited insolence, and studied insult : from the well paid pampered viewer, down to the office of proud keker. We do not wish to express ourselves with any unjust asperity; but smarting, as we are under the lash of accumulated oppression, it is our duty to speak out, and to speak loud enough to be heard, by those who have the power to give us redress. Nor ought we to be accused of impertinence, or improper boldness for so doing : we are MEN and we are BROTHERS. Our capacity for labour, or in other words our physical strength is as much our property, as the land, and coal mines, are the property of our masters. Although from year to year we are fettered with a bond, that ties us down to the most vexations conditions, in the most degrading manner : yet surely we cannot be blamed for thus expressing our sentiments upon our situation, and expressing them in the plainest manner that we are able; we have long found that grumbling is of no use, and that resistance in individual cases is unavailing. We know that it is our prerogative as Englishmen to unite and complain: it is the unalienable right of nature, to demand equity, and "fair play," from all our fellow men, with whom we are connected. Justice is our undoubted right, and no law either human or divine, forbids us endeavouring to obtain it. We think we have taken a fair, honourable, and straight forward course. We have laid our complaints before our masters, without any perverse attempts at intimidation or violence. Without attempting any cessation from labour, as has been our conduct, on former occasions. We want all unfair restrictions removed—we want a fair remuneration for our labour—in a word, we want to procure that, which from the exercise of our skill and labour, we have a right to expect and receive, a decent, comfortable livelihood, for ourselves and families. The coal trade, we have reason to believe, will afford enough for our remuneration, after amply paying for the use of the capital embarked in it by the owners. We are not ignorant of the great expense incurred, in the working of the mine; yet princely fortunes have been amassed, by both our employers and their ancestors; and even men from our own ranks, have grown rich by the emoluments arising from the coal mines; which some consider would be more appropriately named "gold mines." With this however we have nothing to do; as it is our own case we have to consider. And surely it is hard, that we who do the *drudgery;* toil our bodies; *waste* our constitutions; and bring on premature old age, should do all this, for next to nothing. Paupers in the parish work-house, have a lot preferable to ours; for they are fed and clothed, whether they work or lie idle, The gally slave chained at the oar, has his meat and clothes provided. The very Negroes, in the West India plantations, are better fed, better clad, and enjoy more of the pleasures of life, than the pitmen of this district. Surely if the coal-trade will not allow a more liberal system to be acted upon, in reference to our wages, it had much better be given up altogether ; and the pitmen be sent to work, at some of the numerous canals, rail-roads, or turnpikes, that are constructing, in different parts of the kingdom. Or, if these would not afford them employment, the Welsh pits, or *Mexican mines*, might be resorted to ; any thing is better, than the horrid slavery we are doomed to suffer. Suppose a case, (and there are many cases even worse,) a collier, with a wife and three children : is bound for twelve months; and that the best side of our slavery may be seen, that he makes £2. per fortnight : now when he comes to reckon with his overman, he finds that there are so many corves " set out," so many " laid out," so many condemned for " bad separation," that his two notes, which he expected for his labour, are brought down to 34s., and when he adds to this, so much for gunpowder, so much for candles, so much for picks and repairing them, so much for house rent, &c. &c. his wages are then brought down to 30s, for his fortnight's labour : making only 15s, per week, not 6d. a day for himself and each member of his family. Now, let us see how far this will go towards supplying the wants of his family.

	s.	d.
His bread $2\frac{1}{2}$ st. at 2s. 6d. per stone - - -	6	3
1lb. of butcher meat per day, at 7d. per lb. -	4	1
2 pks. of potatoes, at 1s. per peck - - - -	2	0
Oatmeal and milk for 7 breakfasts at $4\frac{1}{2}$d ea.		
morning - - - - - - - - - -	2	8
	15	0

Here the whole sum is expended, without reckoning any thing for clothes : without providing any tea, and supper, or any of those little comforts, that a delicate wife, and sickly children, may be supposed to want: and which should be supplied, on the following scale, to produce any thing like comfort,

	s.	d.
2 oz. of tea at 6d. per oz. - - - - -	1	0
2 lb. of sugar at 8d. per lb. - - - -	1	4
1 lb. salt butter - - - - - - - - -	1	2
1 lb. of cheese - - - - - - - -	0	9
Pepper, salt, mustard and vinegar - -	0	4
Soap, starch, blue, &c. - - - - - -	1	6
Tobacco, $1\frac{1}{2}$ oz. - - - - - - - -	0	$5\frac{1}{4}$
1 pint of ale each day - - - - - -	1	9
Clothing for 5 persons - - - - -	3	0
	11	$3\frac{1}{4}$
Bread, flesh, potatoes, milk and oatmeal, as before stated, -	15	0
	£.1 6	$3\frac{1}{4}$

for meat, drink, and clothing for five persons! Now we would venture to put it to any unprejudiced person, whether this week's provision for 5 persons, is any thing too much, and if any of the individuals composing such family, would fare luxuriously. We are persuaded, that no one will question the moderation of this statement, but allow, that it is nothing but reasonable, that a working man should be placed in circumstances, to enable him to live above *starvation*. It is well known, that many of the colliers would literally die for want, if they did not take their children to work, almost as soon as they can speak and walk. Think what a trial this must be to an intelligent man, to have his dear children immured for 14 hours every day in the gloomy dungeon. How he must deplore the necessity of his situation, which compels him to rob his children of *ease, education* and *comfort,* in order to procure a present and scanty existence. Without thus, doing violence to his feelings, in sending his children to work, he, and the rest of his family, must forego *every* comfort of life. We have seen from the statement of his wages, that sugar, butter, coffee, tea, ale, cheese and several other things, for which he has as much a relish as any other man, are, in many instances, absolutely above his reach. The markets are now looking up, with not even a distant hope of provisions being cheap, as long as the corn bill is in operation, and the bank note system continues ; judge then, what kind of a prospect we have before us.

We appeal then to your honour, as gentlemen ; (which we hope you will not suffer to be tarnished, now that you know our sufferings,) to put an end to a system, so ruinous to us. We appeal to the humane feelings of your nature :—as fellow men, we entreat you. We appeal to you, under the high name of *christianity ;* in the name of the universal Father of mercies ; who distributeth his blessings to the evil and the good : to have compassion upon our situation ; and to step forward in the spirit of justice, equity and brotherly love. Redress our grievances, and make us free. Then shall the blessing of those that are ready to perish come upon you ; and what is still preferable, the blessing of Him who reigneth on high ; which blessing maketh " RICH AND ADDETH NO SORROW WITH IT."

FINIS.

PRINTED BY J. CLARK, JUN., MARKET PLACE, SOUTH SHIELDS.

OBSERVATIONS

ON THE

LAWS RELATING TO THE COLLIERS

𝔎𝔫 𝔖𝔠𝔬𝔱𝔩𝔞𝔫𝔡;

AND

REMARKS ON A BILL

PROPOSED

TO BE BROUGHT INTO PARLIAMENT,

FOR

Regulating the Service, Mode of Hiring, and Rate of Wages,

OF

THE COLLIERS & OTHER PERSONS,

EMPLOYED

IN OR ABOUT THE COAL-WORKS IN SCOTLAND;

𝔓𝔲𝔟𝔩𝔦𝔰𝔥𝔢𝔡 𝔦𝔫 𝔱𝔥𝔢 𝔊𝔩𝔞𝔰𝔤𝔬𝔴 ℭ𝔬𝔲𝔯𝔦𝔢𝔯, 𝔦𝔫 𝔄𝔭𝔯𝔦𝔩, 1799:

TO WHICH ARE ADDED,

A FEW REFLECTIONS

ON THE PRESENT RELATIVE

STATE OF THE COLLIERS & COAL-MASTERS.

GLASGOW:

PRINTED BY JAMES HEDDERWICK AND SON.

1825.

PREFACE.

In the spring of the year 1779, the Coal Proprietors and Coalmasters in the neighbourhood of Edinburgh, brought into Parliament a Bill, which, had it succeeded, would have placed the Colliers in Scotland, in a state of ignominious servitude, not much different from that from which they were emancipated by an Act of the Legislature, in the year 1775.

This measure did not fail to excite an extraordinary sensation over the whole of Scotland; but the most lively interest against it was expressed in the populous Counties of Lanark, Ayr, and Renfrew. The Magistrates and Council of Glasgow, Paisley, and Greenock, the Chamber of Commerce, the Merchants' House and the Trades' House of Glasgow, and all the Coalmasters and many of the Coal Proprietors in the West of Scotland, sent Petitions to Parliament, against the Bill; and strenuous opposition having been made by the whole body of the working Colliers in Scotland, whom the measure was most immediately to affect, the Bill was thrown out, although brought forward and supported by the influence of the then Lord Advocate of Scotland, who was himself an extensive

Coalmaster in the County of Mid Lothian. A short and harmless Bill was passed in its place, declaring that Colliers should be subjected to the same laws and regulations, to which all other labourers were subjected by the laws of Scotland.

The chief grounds of opposition were: first, The direct purpose of the measure to impose unreasonable restraints on one class of workmen, from which all other workmen in Britain were exempted; and, second, Its unavoidable tendency to create a monopoly of the coal trade, in favour of the Coalmasters who were then in possession of that trade, by enslaving the workmen to the existing collieries, and thus preventing an increase of their numbers.

Time effects wonderful changes in the affairs of man. It is only twenty-five years since the Coalmasters in the eastern parts of Scotland, made the above attempt to effect a monopoly, by means of tyranny and slavery, in opposition to public opinion. At the present moment, circumstances are completely reversed. The Colliers in the west of Scotland, have laid, and are at present maturing and extending, an artful plan, to overturn the usual relation between the employer and the employed: to place the control of all the collieries in Scotland, in the hands of the workmen: to enable the workmen to monopolise the working of coal, to the present possessors of that occupation, and their descendants; and to limit or extend the quantities brought to market, so as they may have the power of regulating the rate of wages, according to their own pleasure.

The publication now brought forward, originally made its appearance in one of the Glasgow newspapers, with the view of exciting the voice of the public a-gainst an oppressive and selfish measure, originating with the Coalmasters near Edinburgh. It had, at least, the effect of exciting attention and consideration; and this small work is again offered to the notice of the public, for the purpose of reminding the community of the successful exertions that were made in the year 1799, for protecting the working Colliers from the unreasonable regulations proposed by the Masters, and for calling the public attention to regulations equally unreasonable and prejudicial to the commu-nity, which are now attempted to be carried into ef-fect, by a general association of the workmen.

OBSERVATIONS,

&c.

***

PREVIOUS to the year 1775, all Colliers, and other persons employed at coal-works, were, by the common law of Scotland, in a state of slavery. They and their wives and children, if they had assisted for a certain period at a coal-work, became the property of the Coalmaster, and were transferable with the coal-work, in the same manner as the slaves on a West Indian estate, are held to be property, and transferable on a sale of the estate.

Besides the law founded on the usage of the country, and decisions of the courts, sundry Scotch Statutes were enacted, for regulating this description of labourers.

In particular, by an Act of King James VI. passed in the year 1606;* it was enacted, That no person should hire any Collier, or Coal-bearer, without a sufficient testimonial from the master whom he had last served, or an attestation of a reasonable cause of removal, obtained from a magistrate of the district whence the Collier had come; that any person who

***

* James VI. Parl. 18, cap. 11.

hired a Collier, without such a certificate, should be liable to a penalty, if he did not restore the Collier to the master from whom he had deserted, within twenty-four hours of his being claimed; and, that such Colliers or Coal-bearers, as should receive fore-wages and fees, should be esteemed reputed, holden, and punished as thieves.

This Statute, empowered masters and owners of coal-works, to apprehend all vagabonds and sturdy beggars, and to put them to labour.

By a subsequent Statute, passed in the first Parliament of King Charles II.* the above Statute of James VI. was ratified. And because watermen, who lave and draw water in the coal, or on the pit-head, and labourers, who work on the roads and passages in the pits, were as necessary to the owners and masters of the coal-pits, as the coal-hewers and bearers; it was therefore enacted, That no person should hire any Watermen, Windlasmen, or Gatesmen, without a testimonial from the master whom they had served, under the pains contained in the former Acts. It was declared by this Statute, not to be lawful for any Coalmaster to give a greater fee or bounty to any Collier, than twenty merks Scots (equal to $£1:2:2\frac{8}{12}$ sterling). And it was enacted, that the Colliers, and other workmen in coal-pits, should work all the six days of the week, except during the time of Christmas, under the penalty of twenty shillings Scots, (that is, one shilling and eight pence sterling,) to be

---

* Charles II. Parl. 1, Ses. 1, cap. 56.

paid to their master for each day's absence, besides damages and corporal punishment.

And lastly, when an Act was passed in the year 1701, for preventing the oppression of wrongous imprisonment, and undue delays in trial, it was declared that this salutary Statute should not extend to Colliers.

Such are the regulations which are to be found in the statutory law of Scotland, for keeping in subjection a useful class of the community, whom the mistaken policy of the country thought it necessary to continue in a state of slavery, after every other vestige of personal bondage, resulting from the feudal law, had been abolished.

Independently of the odium attached to a state of perpetual personal servitude, the low rank which the Colliers were doomed to hold in the scale of society, is sufficiently indicated by the whole tenor of these degrading Statutes.

The testimonial or attestation required by the Statute, evidently proceeded from the principle that the Colliers were actually in a state of slavery, and was in effect a letter of emancipation. It was also a regulation, which resulted from this state of bondage, that other Coalmasters should be prohibited from tempting the Colliers to desert, by offering them high bounties; and the circumstance of their being bondmen, made it likewise necessary to have recourse to a coercive law, to compel them to work every lawful day. But it was certainly an aggravation of severity, to enact that they should be punished as thieves, if they should receive wages beforehand from their masters. And it was not less rigorous, to deprive them of the protection afforded to the other subjects of this kingdom, against wrongous imprisonment and undue delays in trial.

The miserable and degraded state, in which Colliers were held by their masters, is likewise demonstrated by the general statutory commission given to Coalmasters, of impressing vagabonds and sturdy beggars into the service of the coal-works.

While such laws as these were allowed to exist, the obvious and unavoidable consequence would be, that the coal-pits would be filled, and the necessary operations performed, by no other persons than vagabonds and lawless banditti.

It will, however, remain as a memorable fact in the history of this country, that these laws did exist in Scotland, till near the end of the eighteenth century, when the Statute of the 15th year of Geo. III. chapter 28, was passed, to relieve the Colliers from the oppression and ignominy of a state of slavery, which reflected so much dishonour on a free country.

The preamble of that Statute is expressed in forcible language, and conveys a full impression of the sentiments then entertained by the Legislature, of this part of our law; it is in these words, " Whereas by the " Statute law of Scotland, as explained by the judges

" of the courts there, many Colliers and Coal-bearers
" and Salters, are in a state of slavery or bondage;
" bound to the collieries or salt-works, where they
" work for life; transferable with the collieries and
" salt-works, when their original masters have no
" farther use for them. And whereas, persons are
" discouraged from learning the art or business of Col-
" liers or Coal-bearers and Salters, by their becoming
" bound to the collieries and salt-works for life, where
" they shall work for the space of one year, by means
" whereof, there are not a sufficient number of Col-
" liers, Coal-bearers, and Salters in Scotland, for
" working the quantities of coal and salt necessarily
" wanted; and many new discovered coals remain
" unwrought, and many are not sufficiently wrought,
" nor are there a sufficient number of Salters for the
" salt-works, to the great loss of the owners, and dis-
" advantage of the public. And whereas, the eman-
" cipating and setting free the Colliers, Coal-bearers,
" and Salters in Scotland, who are now in a state of
" servitude, gradually and upon reasonable conditions,
" and the preventing others from coming into such a
" state of servitude, would be the means of increasing
" the number of Colliers, Coal-bearers, and Salters,
" to the great benefit of the public, without doing any
" injury to the present masters, and would remove
" the reproach of allowing such a state of servitude
" to exist in a free country."

It is therefore enacted, " that from and after the
" first day of July, in the year 1775, no person who
" shall begin to work as a Collier, Coal-bearer, or
" Salter, or in any other way in a colliery or salt-

" work in Scotland, shall be bound to such colliery
" or salt-work, or to the owner thereof, in any way
" or manner different from what is permitted by the
" law of Scotland, with regard to servants and la-
" bourers. And that they shall be deemed free, and
" enjoy the same privileges, rights, and immunities,
" with the rest of his Majesty's subjects, any law or
" usage in Scotland, to the contrary not withstand-
" ing."

The Statute contains various rules for gradually
giving freedom to the Colliers; and, lest there might
remain any doubt as to the extension of the general
clause, conferring the rights, privileges, and immunities of other subjects, to the important privilege of
security against wrongous imprisonment, it concludes
with the following clause:

" And be it farther enacted, that, from and after
" the first day of July 1775, all Colliers, and Salters,
" then free, and all persons that may thereafter be-
" come Colliers, and Salters, and all Colliers, and
" Salters, bound to any colliery or salt-work, upon
" the said first day of July, from the time of obtaining
" their freedom, under the authority of this Act, shall
" be entitled to the benefit of an Act made in the Par-
" liament of Scotland, in the year 1701, entitled, ' An
" Act for preventing wrongous imprisonment, and a-
" gainst undue delays in trials;' any thing in the said
" Act to the contrary not withstanding."

By this Act, the Legislature had it in view, not
only to liberate the Colliers, but to diffuse civilisation

and happiness among them; and, by these means, to give a stimulus to their exertions, and to occasion an increase of their numbers. And this object has been very fully attained. For, in consequence of the freedom thus conferred, not only have the Colliers in Scotland increased twenty-fold, and many new sources of wealth been thereby opened up; but the Colliers themselves have risen rapidly in the scale of society: they are, with very few exceptions, sober and attentive to their business: they are, in general, in the progressive acquisition of property; and many of them, by laudable and spirited exertions, in obtaining education and accumulating wealth, have been enabled to start out of the sphere of operative Colliers, and to become themselves lessees of established coalworks, or of new fields of coal, which their observation and experience have brought into view.

While the Coal Trade in Scotland is thus situated, and not a murmur is heard from the Colliers, or the most remote danger of a mutiny apprehended; and, while the labour of the present Colliers is, in almost all situations in Scotland, sufficient to answer the demands for coal, the Coalmasters in the east part of the kingdom, have judged it prudent to propose, that a Bill should be brought into Parliament, with a view of establishing a variety of legislative restraints and regulations on the Colliers; or rather, with a view of reviving the old slavish regulations of the Scotch Statutes, which were abolished along with the slavery itself, by the Act of the 15th of Geo. III.

Before entering on a consideration of the principle of the proposed Bill, and tendency of its clauses, it will be proper to recapitulate the regulations contained in the Scotch Statutes, and to contrast them with the regulations of this Bill.

By common law, the Colliers were bound servants for life; and the enactments of the Scotch Statutes were, that no person should hire a Collier without a testimonial from his master, or an attestation from a magistrate, of a sufficient cause of removal; and that, if any person hired a Collier, without receiving such certificate, he should incur a penalty. These enactments were extended to all other persons employed in or about the coal-works in Scotland. And it was enacted farther, that no Coalmaster should give a higher bounty than twenty merks to a Collier. And lastly, that the Colliers and other workmen at coal-pits, should work during all the six days of the week, except during the time of Christmas, under the penalty of twenty shillings Scots, to be paid to the master for each day's absence, besides damages and corporal punishment.

By the proposed Bill, all these regulations are to be revived, and several new and more severe restraints to be imposed.

The seventh section of this Bill is in these terms: "That no Coalmaster shall hire any Collier, Coal- "bearer, or other person employed in or about the " coal-works in Scotland, unless they produce to him " a certificate from their last master, bearing that " their former engagement is expired, or a declara- " tion of a judge, that they are at liberty to enter into

" a new engagement. And any Coalmaster hiring or
" engaging any Collier, without such certificate or
" declaration, shall incur a penalty of £50 sterling,
" to be recoverable by summary application to the
" Judge Ordinary, or Court of Session, without the
" power of mitigation."

Here then we are to have the old law against the
hiring or entertainment of slaves revived in its
broadest extent, and applied to the engagement of
free men, with as severe a penalty attached to its
transgression, as if the hiring of a servant were a
crime of the highest magnitude.

While the Collier and his wife and children were
the goods and chattels of the owners of the coal-
works, the law was not thus pointed and severe. It
merely obliged the new employer to restore the de-
serter to his owner within twenty-four hours of being
claimed, and inflicted a penalty upon failure so to
return the Collier. But, by this new regulation, every
Collier must carry in his pocket, a letter of emancipation, or, in other words, a transmission of his person
and service from one master to another, as, without it,
no man will be at liberty to give him employment.

The same section also contains this regulation:
" That no Coalmaster shall be at liberty to engage
" any Collier, at a higher premium or bounty than at
" the rate of one guinea for a year's service."

The Coalmasters in old times, were, by the Scotch
Statutes, allowed to give a bounty of £1 : 2 : $2\frac{8}{12}$.

But this clause with regard to the bounty, is not brought into view for the purpose of founding any thing on the *diminution of bounty*, proposed by the Coalmasters of the present day. Bounties are now deemed a misapplication of money, at almost all the coal-works in Scotland. They are now, with justice, considered to be petty bribes to induce thoughtless men to enter into long contracts of servitude; and the giving and taking of them, is now only practised at those coal-works where the vestiges of the ancient state of servitude are still to be traced. No such practice prevails at the numerous new coal-works that have been established throughout the west of Scotland, where the Colliers are mixed with, and have the habits of, other tradesmen.

It is, however, obvious, that the clause, with regard to bounties, is introduced into the proposed Bill, with the same view for which it was avowedly enacted by the Scotch Statute; viz. to prevent the Colliers from being induced to change their masters.

In the same manner, as the Scotch Statutes contained a clause to compel the Colliers to work six days every week, except during Christmas; so, likewise, does this Bill (section 4th) propose that it should be enacted, That all Colliers, or other persons engaged at any Colliery, shall be obliged to work diligently for six days every week, under the penalty of two shillings and sixpence for every absent day.

On this, and each of the clauses in the Bill, particular observations will be made in the sequel. One general reflection may, however, be here made, with regard to the striking coincidence of regulation appearing between the old and the intended law. The same regulations were originally adopted, nearly two centuries ago, for exacting labour from men in a state of bondage, which are now proposed to be tried for obtaining labour from men in a state of freedom; who, having it in their power to change their profession, if they do not relish the work, and being paid in proportion to their industry, have consequently no inducement to withhold their labour; but, on the contrary, the same incitement as all other freemen to exert their powers for attaining comfort and independence.

From a slight consideration of these regulations, one would be apt to conclude, that they originated in folly, and in a want of due discrimination between the industry of free and bond men; but, when the spirit and principle of the Bill are fairly traced, by an examination of its clauses, the veil is removed; and it appears obvious, that the authors of this measure are the decided enemies of liberty to the Colliers in Scotland; and that the ultimate object of the present attempt is, in effect, to bring back the Colliers to their original bondage, by a Statute disguised under the mask of a measure of policy, and, thereby, to create and preserve a monopoly of the Coal Trade in favour of the present Coalmasters.

Having thus briefly compared the proposed Bill with the ancient Scotch Statutes, we shall next examine the clauses of the Bill, and submit a few observations on each. It will not be necessary to make any remarks on the preamble of the Bill; what has been already advanced, and the observations that follow, show the many errors and absurdities contained in the preamble; and, particularly, the impropriety and injustice of assuming, as facts, many circumstances relating to Colliers, without due inquiry.

The first clause is, That all Colliers in Scotland, who were bound at the passing of the Act of the 15th year of Geo. III, shall be deemed free from their servitude, in the same manner as if they had obtained a decreet of freedom, in the manner directed by that Act.

The Bill, thus, sets out with a clause apparently conferring a favour on the Colliers. But there is, indeed, no favour conferred; for the Act which was passed in 1775, enacted, That all persons who should enter to the business of a Collier, after the first day of July in that year, should be free; and should enjoy the same privileges, rights, and immunities, with the rest of His Majesty's subjects. Twenty-four years having nearly elapsed since that period, nine-tenths of the Colliers in the kingdom have entered into the profession as free men; and all the Colliers still living, who were Colliers at the time that Act was passed, are entitled to obtain decreets of freedom, when they choose to apply to the Sheriffs of the Counties where the works, at which they began their trade, are situated. That Act has also pointed out, very clearly, the mode of obtaining their freedom, and at a small expense.—" It has declared the deci-
" sion of the Sheriff-Courts to be *final*, in order, no

" doubt, to prevent appeals by the Masters to the
" Superior Courts, where, the poverty of the men
" pursuing for their freedom, would expose them to
" be borne down by the power of their employers.
" This distinction is just. It marks the liberality of
" those who introduced the Bill into Parliament, and
" does honour to the Legislature for having adopted
" their ideas."—(See *Letter to Coalmasters*, Edin.
1787.)

The second clause is of the following import: That
the Justices of the Peace in each County, shall be empowered to regulate the wages of all Colliers and
Coal-bearers, and all workmen employed in the collieries, whether in coal-hewing and coal-bearing, or
in any other work in or about collieries; and, that a
quorum of the said Justices shall, when required,
and at least once in the year, fix the rates of wages
at which the said Colliers, Coal-bearers, or others,
shall be bound to work, and their Masters shall be
bound to pay these rates; and to fix different rates
of wages, according to the nature of the work: but,
it shall be competent, nevertheless, either to the
Coalmaster, Collier, Coal-bearer, or other workman,
at any time, to make special application to the said
Justices, for having the common rates of wages either
raised or lowered, according to the circumstances of
the case.

Every person versant in the business of a coal-
work, will readily admit, that a new branch of duty is
thus provided for the Justices of the Peace, as intri-
cate and difficult as any which has hitherto been im-

posed upon them. Few Colliers in Scotland have, as yet, risen to such a rank in society as might give them a chance of being commissioned as Justices of the Peace; and, however well informed the Justices may be in the laws of their country, and well qualified to apply them to cases in general, yet, so much do the circumstances attending the operation of mining coals, vary in different counties in Scotland, and in the same county at different times, that none but Colliers, can be competent judges of the rate of wages which ought to be paid to the workers of coal.

The Justices of the Peace would, no doubt, have it in their power to go below ground to inspect the Colliers' operations. But, it is believed, that it would not be an easy matter to procure a quorum in each county to take that trouble. And, although Justices were to be found, who would, for once, disregard the inconvenience of exploring the operations of a coal-pit throughout passages, in many cases, only two feet in height, and in an unwholesome atmosphere, at a depth of four or five hundred feet under ground; it is believed that, unless they made a daily practice of such visits, they would, in general, return not much better informed than before they went down.

There are few Coalmasters who have themselves been Operative Colliers, and who can form a practical calculation of the rate of labour; and, there is such a diversity of occurrences in the working of coal, that the most experienced Coalmaster considers it the most difficult branch of his department, to form an accurate estimate of the price of the various pieces of labour. In all coal-works, there is a constant fluctuation of the rate of working, and of the expenses attendant on the various operations; the causes of which will be immediately explained.

At present, the Coalmaster fixes the wages of his men, in some measure, by a comparison of the rates, at which similar pieces of work had previously been performed. But there is such a variety of circumstances, which make work more difficult or more easy in the execution, that it is impossible for any Coalmaster to trust to his own judgment and experience. An obvious difficulty under which he labours, arises from the circumstance, that he cannot, with the same facility as in operations above ground, make his observations upon the activity and industry of different men performing similar contracts.

In all the coal-works in Scotland, there are one, two, or more men in every coal-pit, who act as overseers, and are called Oversmen; whose duty is, to see that the operations are regularly conducted and the work executed, agreeably to the orders of the Master. These Oversmen are, with few exceptions, mere Operative Colliers, and perform the same work as any other Collier in the pit. Besides this duty of attending to the regularity of the work, they also assist the Coalmaster; and sometimes act as umpires between him and the men, in fixing the price of each particular piece of work that occurs.

At all coal-works, there are also many other men employed, in whom the Coalmasters repose so much confidence, as to ask and follow their advice, in any question that occurs with the men, relating to wages, or in any other circumstance attending the work. And it is a well-known fact, that at all the Collieries in Scotland, contracts are entered into between the Coalmasters and the Colliers, and disputes prevented or determined, through the medium of prudent Operative Colliers of the above description; who act as a check upon others more intemperate, or more disposed to impose on the Coalmaster's inexperience.

But, though wages are thus regulated by the master, and submitted to with cheerfulness by the workmen, it is proposed by this Bill, that the Coalmasters should abandon the mode hitherto practised, of settling the rates of wages by the assistance of their confidential servants; and that the Coalmasters and Colliers should commit that part of their trade to a quorum of the Justices of the Peace.

If the masters and their workmen are agreed upon the rate of wages, the appeal to the Justices for their sanction to the agreement will be a very innocent, and, at the same time, a very useless process. But, should a Court of Justices be ever resorted to, where they were at variance, the consequences would be ruinous. From the moment that the master and his servants, impressed with opposite views, resorted to a Court of Law, every sentiment of confidence between them would be destroyed. The Colliers would appear in Court as parties in a law-suit; and, although the most rational and well-principled men at the work were examined as witnesses, with regard to the rates at which wages ought to be paid, their testimony would swerve to the side of their fellow-workmen. They would not, in that case, stand as candid, unbiassed servants, endeavouring to make a friendly bargain with their master; but would appear at the bar of the Court, tinged with the spirit of the litigants.

Yet, the evidence of Operative Colliers appears to be the only evidence, that a Court could resort to, for fixing the rates of the various pieces of work that occur in a pit. No other men could give an opinion on the subject, which could be regarded; and, therefore, it would be on their evidence alone, that the Justices could form their judgment, upon points which they could not themselves understand; and, if the decision were to be given agreeably to the evidence, the probable chance is, that it would be unfavourable to the Coalmaster. Because, it can hardly be supposed, that the Colliers would agree to accept of the same rate of wages, after being irritated by a lawsuit, that they would have accepted, by an amicable compromise before such a proceeding.

And, after all, although candid and disinterested evidence were to be given, with regard to the rate of wages at which the work ought to be performed, and a decision to be pronounced satisfactory to both parties; yet the master and his Colliers would be left just where they were, before they went into Court. They would only hear the Justices ratify a decision, which they themselves could have made, and had been in use to make, at home, without the risk of rancour or animosity. And therefore, in every view of the matter, supposing the Justices of the Peace could be created Colliers by Statute, so as to understand the nature of the various cases that might be laid before them; and, supposing a quorum could, at all times, be found to attend to and regulate the wages, according to the daily fluctuation of the operations in a coal-pit, their interference would either be dangerous or useless. It would be dangerous, in so far as it would tend to destroy the confidence that at present subsists between the masters and their servants, and to shut up the channels of information which the masters at present possess. It would be useless, if the Masters and the Colliers had agreed between themselves, and did not require the sanction of the Justices.

But, with regard to the Justices of the Peace ever attempting to make themselves masters of the price of labour in a coal-pit, or to attend to the variety of work that occurs there daily, it is obviously impossible. This will appear evident, from the following short account of the nature of the work, which, however, being drawn up on the hurry of the present occasion, cannot be supposed to contain all the minute circumstances, or even the outline, of the modes of working coal at some of the coal-works in Scotland.

Colliers are paid for their labour, according to the quantity of coals which they turn out. At many coal-works in Scotland, the Collier not only cuts the coal from the solid stratum, technically termed the coal-wall; but draws it, either by himself or by boys, to the bottom of the pit, in a tub or hutch, made of wood or wicker-work, and placed on wheels, or constructed in the form of a sledge. Where no impediment occurs, to occasion greater difficulty and additional labour in cutting, drawing, or carrying the coal, the rate, per tub or hutch, varies according to the length to which the workings extend from the bottom of the pit.

In many other coal-works, the Colliers only cut the coal from the solid, and fill it into the tub or basket; and this is drawn to the bottom of the pit by horses, kept at the Master's expense. In these cases, the Colliers are also paid, according to the quantity of coals which they cut or loosen from the solid stratum.

In all cases where coal is wrought at a fixed rate for the tub or basket, it is an agreement, that these shall contain a given weight of coal; and, at many works, it is a regulation, that the weight or measure given by the Collier, shall be more full and ample than that by which the coals are sold by the Coalmaster to the public.

At other coal-works, it is not the practice to pay the workmen either by the weight, or measure of the coal in tubs; but according to the solid contents of the stratum cut by the Colliers; or, in other words, in proportion to the excavation made in the seam of coal.

At all the coal-works in Scotland, the price of

working, varies with the character of the strata and the quality of the coal. Many of the seams of coal now wrought, are under two feet in thickness; but, in general, they extend from two to six feet. There are, however, coal strata of far greater thickness. One remarkable instance of this kind, occurs in the work of George Houston, Esq. of Johnston, as lessee of Mr. MacDowall of Garthland, where the coal is about one hundred feet thick. This work is carried on in different floors or stories, by leaving part of the coal for a roof and pavement, and placing the pillars of the upper, precisely above the pillars in the under, floors.

Coals are also of various degrees of hardness or softness. Some are denominated free, and are easily broken by the pick-axe and hammer; others are hard and tenacious. Some are without any mixture of foreign substances; while others contain beds or balls of free-stone, iron-stone, and other minerals. Some lie in regular beds, and have frequent fissures; while others are bound together without either bed or fissure, and have the appearance of a solid mass of melted metal. And it is a well-known fact, that, on the same stratum of coal, and even in the same pit, all those varieties of quality and disposition frequently occur. On these accounts, therefore, the rate of wages, and the allowances to the Colliers for difficult work, are subject to daily change.

Besides these causes of fluctuation, arising from the nature of the coal itself, there are many circumstances attending its working, which impede the operations of the Collier, and affect his wages. For example, the stratum above the coal is frequently insufficient for a roof, and either falls or must be taken down after the coal is excavated; or, where the removal of this would occasion too laborious an operation, it is supported by props of timber and buildings of stone.

At some coal-works, the expense of supporting insufficient roofs, or clearing away the rubbish which they occasion, is laid upon the price of working the coal; and the Colliers, in that case, are obliged to keep the roads, or access to and from the coal-wall, at all times clear. In other cases, the clearing away of falls from the roof, gives constant employment to a number of men kept for that purpose. But, most commonly, the expense of this operation, is paid by extra wages to the Collier; as, in many cases, it is difficult to fix any precise sum, or general rule of charge for it.

It also frequently happens, that the coal is wrought towards the dip, that is, in a descending direction from the bottom of the pit. In these situations, extra wages are also paid, on account of the difficulty of drawing the coal up an acclivity.

It is, likewise, sometimes necessary to work the coal in close mines; where the Collier has not the freedom of an open hand, or, what he terms, cut coal on either side. He is thus obliged to cut, or shear the coal, (as he terms it,) on each side; which renders his work more difficult. And in these situations, as well as in many other operations in coal-pits, it often happens that the air is not ventilated, and, therefore, insufficient to allow a full day's work: allowances must also be made for these difficulties.

Some situations, in the same coal, are also often wet; while others are dry and comfortable. An extra price must, therefore, be paid to the Colliers in the wet situations, according to the circumstances of the case.

Besides all these, and other ordinary occurrences in working coal, there are others of greater importance, of which it is difficult to form any estimate; such as, where the coal disappears in whole or in part, and a different stratum of mineral appears in its place. In these cases, the coal is traced, sometimes upwards and sometimes downwards, by mines, cut through solid stone, and varying in length from one to twenty, thirty, or forty yards. In sinking coal-pits, the ease or difficulty with which the operation can be executed, like the searching for coal under ground, is also various, according to circumstances; such as the hardness or softness of the strata intersected by the workmen, and the quantity of water with which they are burdened.

It is impossible, therefore, to fix a general rate of wages for the operations of a coal-pit. It might as well be proposed, that the Justices of the Peace should fix the rent which a lessee ought to pay to the proprietor; as that they should determine the various minutiæ of expense, which the Coalmaster should incur in the course of his trade. It would also appear, that there is as much reason and necessity for the interference of the Legislature, to establish rules for fixing the price at which the Coalmasters ought to sell their coals to the public; as for fixing the rates at which these ought to be furnished, and other operations performed by the Colliers to the Coalmasters.

The third clause of the Bill bears, That it shall be lawful for any Coalmaster, considering himself aggrieved by the rates of wages affixed by the Justices, or paid to the Colliers, Coal-bearers, or others, though in a different county from that in which the colliery belonging to such Coalmaster is situated, to complain, summarily, to the Court of Session against any other Coalmaster who has paid these rates of wages; and that Court is authorised to review the proceedings of the Justices, and determine what rates of wages shall be paid by the person complained on.

It might be a sufficient objection to this regulation, that every man ought to be allowed to carry on his trade, and to pay his servants agreeably to his pleasure; and that his own interest would direct him, not to pay higher wages than the produce of his trade could afford. It may also be observed, that this clause of the Bill would put it in the power of a wealthy and troublesome proprietor of a coal-work, to oppress, and even crush, by means of law-suits, the owners of collieries of smaller value.

But, farther, the clause has another more pointed and ruinous tendency. It is calculated to cramp industry and fetter exertion, on the part of the Collier; as well as on the part of the Master.

There are many seams of coal now working in Scotland, so thin; or so burdened with water, or infested with mephitic and inflammable air; or attended with such other inconveniencies in the working; that nothing, except higher wages, would induce men to work in these, in preference to others less troublesome.

But the local situation of these coals is, in many cases, so advantageous for the market, that the owners can afford to pay the men higher wages than are paid at neighbouring coal-works, less troublesome in the working, but, at the same time, less favoured in point of situation. It is obvious, that, in the end, both owners may be equal gainers; or, the owner of a seam of coal labouring under the above disadvantages in working, may be content with a small profit, rather than receive no profit at all by allowing his coal to remain unwrought. But the clause now under consideration, militates more especially against those smaller collieries, many of which have been set a-going, and many more of which may yet be established in Scotland; but all of which may, by this enactment, be crushed, in their rivalship of more extensive works.

This clause is, besides, founded in injustice; as no man ought to be prevented from paying for the produce of the labourers he employs, according to his own views of their merits, formed either from a con-

sideration, of the difficulty of the labour, or, of the
skill or despatch with which it is performed to answer the ends which the employer has in view. It
also tends to prevent the exercise of every generous
or benevolent affection of a master towards his servant; for, the master may be dragged to the Court
of Session, for acts of kindness towards worthy, faith-
ful, and deserving servants, by persons who know not
the motives by which he may have been actuated.

By the fourth clause of the Bill, it is enacted,
" That all Colliers, or other persons aforesaid, en-
" gaged at any colliery, shall be obliged to work
" diligently at the said colliery for six days every
" week, during the whole space of their respective
" engagements, at the rates of wages that shall be
" fixed by the Justices, or by the Court of Session,
" as aforesaid, under the penalty of two shillings and
" sixpence sterling for every day they may respec-
" tively absent themselves or fail to work: the said
" penalty to be recoverable before the Justices, with
" full costs; declaring, however, that, in case of sick-
" ness, or any unavoidable accident happening to the
" work, or other just cause, no penalty shall be in-
" curred; and excepting, also, the ancient and accus-
" tomed holidays."

By this enactment for compelling labour, it will
be observed, that the only respite from daily labour
that the Collier can command, is, during the attacks
of his own bodily infirmity, and during what are de-
signated in the Bill, by the vague and indefinite ap-
pellation of ancient and accustomed holidays.

With regard to unavoidable accidents happening
to the work, or other just cause, though these are
introduced as mitigations of this coercive regulation,
and on account of which, no penalty is to be exacted;
these circumstances are clumsily introduced into the
Bill, not as an indulgence to the Colliers, but by way
of covering the Coalmasters from any claim on the
part of the Colliers, on account of being thrown idle.

The intended Act, like other laws, ought to be
founded on principles of equity; while it benefits the
Master, it ought to support the Collier. This, however, is not the case; for it will be noticed, that the
Bill does not contain any enactment, that the Coalmasters throughout Scotland shall be bound to provide work for the Colliers during all the six days of
the week; nor does it subject these Masters in a penalty to the Colliers, for every day's idleness that may
be occasioned through the ignorance, inattention, or
other fault of them or the managers of their works.
In illustration of this part of the subject, it must be
here observed, that, at many valuable and extensive
coal-works, when the sales decline, particularly
during summer, it is a common practice for Masters
to restrict their Colliers to work only four or five
days in the week. Is the Collier to obtain no redress for being thus thrown idle? It may be likewise asked, What provision is made for the Colliers,
if, through the unskilfulness or parsimony of the
Master, the machinery should become insufficient,
and the pits be filled with water, so as not to admit
them to work? What provision is made for them,
when days occur so stormy that the men and horses

above ground, cannot stand to receive the coals, which the workmen are ready to furnish?

An enactment to provide work for the Collier, would, at least, have given the clause under consideration a colour of equity; as it would have been a reciprocal obligation between the Collier, to perform his work, and the Master, at all times, to find work.

But the framers of the Bill seem to have been aware of the danger of introducing such an enactment, from a consciousness that the idle days at the coal-works more frequently originate with the Masters themselves, or those persons to whom the charge of the work is committed, than from the Operative Colliers.

But, in another point of view, this clause, when connected with another relative to the period of the Colliers' servitude, is still more oppressive. It is a marked and coercive enactment against a particular profession; it makes the Colliers indented servants by Statute-law, though they are paid only in proportion to their labour; and it debars them from all recreation, and from the exercise of civil and religious duties in society. By this clause, the Colliers would be denied any relaxation from labour, and the indulgence in their usual recreations on a market-day, or at a marriage-party. They would not be allowed leisure to attend to their concerns, on the occasions of a birth or of a death in their families; they would not be allowed time to settle their children in schools, or their sons at trades, or their daughters in marriage; they would not be allowed to go to mar-

E

ket for provisions, except after the hours of labour; they would not be allowed to visit a relation in a distant part of the country, or attend on a dying friend; nor would they be allowed to attend to the religious institutions of the country. For, as already observed, from the way in which the words " other just cause" are introduced, they are solely applicable to causes occurring to the colliery, and not to the private concerns of the Colliers.

But, even if the words *other just cause* were applicable to the circumstances of the Collier, it may be asked; Who are to be the judges, and by what mode of proof are the Colliers to establish, that they were absent in consequence of a just cause? When sickness, or any of these causes, occurs, are they to call a physician and other witnesses to bear testimony of the justice of their absence from work? Or, by what mode shall they screen themselves from any future oppressive claim for statutory penalties, which the Masters may choose to make?

A moment's attention will show, that the Colliers would be placed in a very hopeless situation, under such a clause, which appears to be one, calculated for no other end, than to place them, entirely, under the arbitrary will of their Masters; and the consequence of which would be, that, by incurring the statutory penalty of 2s. 6d. for each absent day, every Collier in Scotland would, in a short time, be involved so deeply in debt to his Master, as to entail on himself perpetual servitude.

It is no satisfaction to say, that the masters would not rigidly put in force such a regulation. It is enough to object, that the master should not have it in his power to enforce a regulation of such a tendency.

It may also be argued by the friends of the Bill, that hired servants, for farming purposes, are obliged to work six days. But these servants are not paid in proportion to their work; they receive a fixed salary. Besides, their engagement is voluntary; and farm-servants may, if they choose, (and they frequently do,) engage at daily or weekly services. But the Colliers' servitude being to be imposed by Statute, they have no alternative. They must either change their profession, or submit to have their labour regulated by the Statute.

It may be farther observed, that the labour of a Collier and the labour of a farm-servant are widely different. That of the latter is mere recreation, compared to the labour of the former; who, being paid for his labour according to the quantity of work performed, and being secluded from society and the light of the sun when performing his work, is, by these circumstances, unconsciously impelled to work with a degree of vigour unknown in any other profession. Indeed, such is the excessive severity of this labour, that it is generally allowed, that the human constitution could not support it above five days in the week. This, it will readily be believed, must, in a particular manner, be the case in seams from two feet to thirty inches in thickness; where the Colliers are obliged to bend their bodies nearly double, to accommodate themselves to the lowness of the roof.

Before leaving this part of the Bill, it must also be noticed, that children of both sexes, from six to twelve or fourteen years of age, and married and unmarried women, are employed as bearers of coal. But, without any regard to humanity, women and children are, by a special enactment, included under this coercive regulation of six days' servitude, without indulgence or regard to family duties, which may necessarily require the attention of the women, and without any allotment of time for the education of the children.

An inhabitant of a free and civilized country, would read of the existence of such a law among a nation of barbarians, with feelings of emotion; and yet, a law of this nature is now to be proposed to the British Legislature.

By the 5th section of the Bill, it is enacted, "That " every Collier or other, as aforesaid, who either now " is working, or shall hereafter lawfully engage to " work, at any colliery, (having no previous engage- " ment,) shall be bound to continue working at the " same colliery, for six months, at the wages to be " fixed by the Justices aforesaid." And, by the 7th section, it is enacted, "That no Coalmaster shall hire " any Collier, Coal-bearer, or other, as aforesaid, " unless they produce to him a certificate from their " last Master, bearing, that their former engagement " is expired; which certificate, every Coalmaster shall

" be bound to grant, at the expiry of such Collier's
" or other person's engagement, under the penalty
" of ten pounds sterling. And, in case of refusal,
" it shall be competent to the Collier to apply to
" the Judge Ordinary, or Justices of Peace for the
" County, to be declared at liberty to enter into a
" new engagement; which declaration, the said Judge
" Ordinary, or Justices, shall be obliged to grant,
" unless the said Coalmaster can show that the en-
" gagement is not expired. And any Coalmaster
" hiring or engaging any Collier, Coal-bearer, or
" other, as aforesaid, without such certificate or de-
" claration, shall incur a penalty of fifty pounds ster-
" ling to the Coalmaster whose service the Collier
" had left; and such engagement shall be null and
" void, to all intents and purposes: the said pen-
" alty of fifty pounds sterling, with full costs of suit,
" to be recoverable by summary application to the
" Sheriff-Depute, or Stewart-Depute, or to the Court
" of Session, without the power of mitigation. Pro-
" vided, always, that such Collier, &c. shall be bound,
" before receiving such certificate, to give six weeks
" previous warning, in writing, to his Master, of his
" intention to leave his service when the period of
" his engagement expires; and that such Coalmaster,
" within eight days after receiving such notification,
" shall be bound to grant to such Collier, an acknow-
" ledgment that he has received such notice, and that
" he is free at the expiry of his term."

No person, who reads these clauses, need hesitate
a moment in making a conclusion, with regard to
the object they have in view. It is obvious, that

they are calculated for no other purpose than to prevent the free circulation of the labour of Colliers, or, in other words, to bind them completely to their present Masters, under the mask of a legislative act of policy.

For, independently of the direct obligation in the Bill, that every Collier is to enter upon six months servitude from the time of passing the Act, and for the same period from the date of his entry to every other work, he is obliged to sue for his freedom, and to obtain liberty of engaging with another Master, by so circuitous a process, that an illiterate man never would attempt it; and those, who did attempt to obtain their freedom, would be involved in lawsuits, upon claims made by the Masters for the statutory penalties on account of absent days, which the Colliers might not be able to prove by witnesses, were occasioned by sickness.

But, the enactment on this point imposes such a restraint on personal liberty, and so pointedly marks out Colliers, as a different class in society from any other labourer, that it would be highly inexpedient, even for the present Masters, to propose any such statutory restraints.

In a state of freedom, where men enjoy equal rights and privileges, any coercive statutory regulation, tending to mark out a particular profession, as requiring stricter legislative enactments for their conduct than others of the community, would obviously throw an odium on that profession; and, independently of the general prejudice, which would thus be entertained by other mechanics against such a profession, the Colliers themselves would be in a continued state of irritation, arising from the reflection, that their labour was to be exacted from them by compulsion, and that they were precluded by Statute from changing their Masters, like other labourers and mechanics. They could not feel the same motives to industry and exertion, with men who have an unlimited choice of their employers.

The inevitable consequence of coercive laws is, a mutinous disposition in those against whom they are enacted; and, were those regulations adopted which are proposed, for exacting from the Colliers six days work under penalties for absence, and six months servitude without the liberty of going away, except by a tedious and formal liberation, it would be their daily study to evade or defeat them. They would excite stubbornness and cunning in some, and outrage in others; and, in all, a want of that hearty exertion which is uniformly the result of a free choice.

The Colliers would thus fall back into their original state of ignorance; they would be ready, on all occasions, to mutiny, or take advantage of their Masters; and an unavoidable diminution of their numbers would take place. Strangers would be debarred from beginning the profession, not only by the statutory restraints imposed upon it, but by the forbidding customs and manners of the people already in the trade, resulting from these regulations; and thus, not only a deficiency of regular labour, but a scarcity of men, would be the consequence.

In another view of the matter, these regulations are inexpedient; because they would have the effect, in some measure, of perpetuating the service of the present Colliers with their present Employers.

By the Bill, it is proposed, that all Colliers should be bound to every work at which they might begin to labour, for six months from the date of their entry. A Collier, therefore, would, in most cases, rather submit to inconvenience, and even injustice, with his present Employer, than go away; when he knew that he could not be taken into any other work, except under a bondage of six months. In many cases, likewise, Colliers have been involved in debt by the policy of their Masters, in order to bind them to their works; and, by this Bill, another source of incurring debt is provided, viz.: by the penalties to which the Colliers are to be subjected by absence from work. The Bill contains a clause (section 6th) to deter Coalmasters, who may be in want of men, from advancing money to Colliers, under a certification of its not being recoverable; and, therefore, no Collier, who has involved himself in debt, either by fair contraction, or by penalties, could extricate himself on any emergency, when an opportunity offered of making an advantageous change of his situation.

But, besides all these impediments to a Collier's free choice of changing his Employer, he is obliged, to carry about his manumission, at all times when he wants employment. With a troublesome and ill-natured Master, the Collier would, at all times, find it difficult to procure this letter of liberation; and, independently of the evil consequences to the public, that would result from any plan that may be adopted for imposing restraints on the Collier's free choice of a Master, and of a coal-work, the proposed regulations are arbitrary and unjust, in as far as they mark out a particular class of the community, who have not a free and unreserved disposal of their own persons; but must produce a manumission from their last Master, before they can obtain employment from another.

There are no regulations of this kind existing in Great Britain, with respect to any other profession; and, if such regulations were adopted with regard to the Colliers, they would appear to be the forerunners of similar restraints, for all those employed at other mechanical or laborious employments in the kingdom. The present manufacturers of all kinds of goods and merchandise, might, with the same propriety, propose to bring a Bill into Parliament, for binding their operatives under similar servitude and legislative restraint. But such an attempt would be viewed with just indignation, as a flagrant attack on the personal liberty of the subject; and the measure, now proposed by the Masters in a particular trade, not only amounts to a violation of liberty, but is obviously calculated to secure a monopoly of the labour of the Operative Colliers, and, consequently, of the coal trade, to the present Coalmasters.

The public at large are, therefore, deeply interested in this question; because all monopolies have for their object, an unfair rise in the price of the article

F

monopolised; and every proprietor of unwrought coal is individually interested, as the proposed law will prevent him from procuring hands to work that coal, except by very slow degrees.

By the 6th section of the Bill, a long set of regulations is introduced, with regard to debts owing by the Colliers; and to prevent Coalmasters from advancing money, in the view of transmitting the services of Colliers from one Master to another.

These regulations with regard to old debts, afford some proof of a practice, which has prevailed since the Act of 1775, of making the Colliers bound servants, by keeping them involved in debt and bankruptcy. That practice is happily wearing away in many parts of the kingdom, by the progressive advancement of the Colliers in knowledge and independence; and, it is to be hoped, that, at no distant period, this disgraceful and pernicious mode of enslaving and debasing men, will disappear from Scotland. It would, indeed, be a wise and expedient legislative measure to prevent it.

But the immediate and principal object of the 6th section of the Bill is, to prevent the Colliers from receiving credit with a new Master to enable them to extricate themselves from debt due to another.

In one point of view, the object of this clause is proper; as it is calculated to prevent traffic in men, by a mortgage or pledge of their service: but, in another view of the matter, it appears to have been dictated by the same principle as the rest of the Bill—for the purpose of perpetuating the services of the Colliers with their present Employers; as it puts it out of their power to ask assistance from any other Master, to relieve them from debt, either fairly contracted, or incurred by the statutory penalties for absent days.

The only other section of the Bill which requires to be noticed, is the 8th; by which, Colliers are to be prevented from enlisting into His Majesty's army or navy.

This clause also contains a restraint on the voluntary action of the Colliers, which serves to distinguish them from all other classes in the community, and is, therefore, unjust and invidious; and, although it were not subject to this objection, it is liable to another. It does not provide, that the Colliers may not be ballotted as militiamen; and, if they are to be debarred in future, from entering, as volunteers, into the service of their country, they ought not to be exposed to the chance of being required to serve against their will.

To conclude, by the Act of 1775 certain privileges have been conferred on the Scotch Colliers; or, rather, the rights of humanity have been asserted, and a reproachful servitude abolished from this free country.

Why withdraw from the Colliers the rights so lately conferred? Have they been turbulent, or shown themselves unworthy of the liberty they enjoy? Why impose upon Colliers in Scotland, obligations and restrictions which do not exist in England? "There, "the Colliers are free. The very air of that country, "equally inimical to slavery and to tyrants, sets at "liberty, on his first landing, even the unhappy "African, though recently purchased with the gold of "his European master."* Now, as Scotland and England are one kingdom, the Collier in the North ought to enjoy the same freedom with his neighbour in the South. The 4th article of the Union expressly says, "That there be communication of all rights and "privileges which do or may belong to the subjects "of either kingdom, except where it is otherwise "agreed to in these articles." But, will the Collier in Scotland, by the proposed Bill, be upon a footing with the Collier in England? No. The probable, the evident consequences of the Bill will be, to diminish the number of Colliers by driving them to England, where there are no restraints. This is worthy of the serious consideration of Coalmasters in Scotland; and it is a sufficient reason against the adoption of any regulation, that it does not also exist in England.

The good effects of the Act 1775 have been experienced. The emancipation of the Colliers has not only answered the humane and benevolent intentions of the Legislature; but has, also, been attended with advantages to the Coalmasters. The rates of Colliers' wages have advanced, in proportion to the wages of other labourers and tradesmen. Freed now from a

---

* Letter to Coalmasters in Scotland. Edin. 1787.

state of bondage, they perform more work, and exert themselves more strenuously for their Masters' benefit. At some coal-works in the west, when an extraordinary demand for fuel has occurred, the Colliers, working by turns, and relieving one another, have kept the same pit going night and day without cessation, for several weeks, or months. Their number is increased; their deportment is regular; and they are, in most instances, men of sobriety. It is not, therefore, to be supposed, that the Legislature will counteract the good effect of this salutary Statute, by recurring to laws analogous to the ancient Scottish Statutes relating to Colliers and Salters; especially, as every man who became a Collier within these last twenty-four years, entered upon the profession, under the impression, and with the firm conviction, that the former state of servitude was for ever abolished.

Such are the reflections which have occurred, on a short consideration of the proposed Bill; and which have been drawn up in haste, in opposition to a measure which may be attended with serious national consequences. And, as it is generally understood, that many of the Coalmasters in Scotland disapprove of the Bill; and that few of them, and none of the Colliers, have had an opportunity of considering it: it would appear to be, at least, prudent to delay bringing it into Parliament, until the sense of all parties interested be fairly taken.

IN consequence of the opposition made to this extraordinary Bill, and of the opinions expressed by the members of the Committee of the House of Commons, to whom it was remitted, the Lord Advocate of Scotland and the other Coalmasters of Mid-Lothian, by whom it had been brought forward, abandoned the measure; and, in its place, a Bill was carried through Parliament, in the month of June 1799, entitled, " An " Act to explain and amend the laws relative to Col- " liers, in that part of Great Britain called Scotland;" of which the following are the leading enactments:

I. That, from and after the passing of the said Act, all the Colliers in that part of Great Britain called Scotland, who were bound Colliers, at the time of passing the Act of the 15th year of the reign of George III., should be, and they are thereby declared to be, free from their servitude, and in the same situation in every respect, as if they had regularly obtained a decree, in the manner directed by the said Act.

II. That the Acts of the Scottish Parliament, James VI. (28th June 1617) chapter 8th, and Charles II. (1st January 1661) chapter 38, in so far as the same relate to the fixing and appointing of the ordinary hire and wages of labourers, workmen, and servants, do extend to, and include Colliers, Coal-hewers, Coal-bearers, and all other persons of every description employed at collieries, in that part of Great Britain called Scotland.

III. That the powers and authorities for fixing and appointing hire and wages, should only be exercised, upon the application of the party or parties aggrieved.

IV. That any two or more Justices, might, and should, exercise, upon application made to them, all the powers and authorities which are given, by the aforesaid Statutes, to the Justices at their Quarter-Sessions, in such manner as is therein provided.

V. That, whereas, there was a general practice, a-mong the Coal-owners and Lessees of coal, of advancing considerable sums to their Colliers, or for their behoof, much beyond what the Colliers were able to repay; which sums were advanced, for the purpose of tempting them to enter into or continue their engagements, notwithstanding the sums so advanced, were kept up as debts against the Colliers; it was, therefore, enacted, that no diligence, or action, should be competent for any sum, or sums, thereafter to be lent, or advanced, to Colliers, or other persons employed at the collieries, as aforesaid, by the Coal-owner or Lessee of any colliery, or by any other person or persons on their behalf; or for any debts due by Colliers, or other persons, as aforesaid, which should be acquired by the said Coal-owners or Lessees, or by others on their account, either previous to their engagement, or during the currency thereof, and in view of the same; excepting, always, such sum, or sums, as should be advanced to any Collier, or other persons employed at collieries, as aforesaid, during the currency of his, or her,* service, for the support of his, or her, family, in case of sickness.

VI. That it should, and might, be lawful to the Coal-owner or Lessee, who should lend or advance such sum, or sums, of money, to retain, from the wages of the Colliers or others aforesaid, one-twelfth part of the said sums weekly, till the principal sum, without interest, be paid up; declaring, that, if the engagement of such Collier should expire before the principal sum so advanced was fully paid up, the Coal-owner or Lessee who advanced the same, should have action for the balance, in the same manner as if the said Act had not passed.

VII. That such debts as were due by Colliers to their Masters, at or before the passing of the Act, should not be thereby extinguished.

VIII. That all persons seducing, or attempting to seduce, Colliers or others aforesaid from the kingdom of Great Britain, should be punished in the same manner as persons seducing, or attempting to seduce, Manufacturers or Artisans, are punishable by law.

IX. That no Coalmaster, or Lessee of coal, should act as a Justice of Peace under that Act.

X. That the laws then in force, against unlawful combinations of whatever kind, should extend to,

---

* The barbarous practice of employing women in collieries is here referred to.

and include, Colliers, Coal-bearers, and other persons
employed at coal-works, as aforesaid; and, that
nothing in the Act should extend to, alter, or repeal,
any part of the Acts of the Parliament of Scotland;
unless so far as was expressly done by the said Act, or
by the Act of the 15th year of the reign of Geo. III.

By this Act, the Colliers were placed on the same
footing, and in the same freedom in the exercise of
their trade, with other labourers. Restrictions,
indeed, still remained; but these attached not to the
Colliers alone, but to every class of workmen in the
kingdom.

Under the system of laws now established, the
Colliers maintained their equality with other labourers, and continued to improve in character and condition. The laws against unlawful combinations existed in their fullest vigour; and yet, the wages of
the Colliers continued to advance. At the passing of
the last mentioned Act in 1799, the ordinary rate of
their wages, in the west of Scotland, was four shillings a-day; and the coal trade was in a state of
progressive improvement. Shortly afterwards, wages
were advanced, at many of the collieries around
Glasgow, to five shillings a-day; and at that rate
they continued till the year 1815 or 1816. Then
they experienced a reverse. From 1817 to 1823, they
gradually fell, until, in the latter year, they were no
higher than three shillings and sixpence a-day. In
some of these years, too, particularly in 1819, 1820,
and 1821, the demand for coal had so greatly diminished, that the working period, at many of the col-

lieries, was restricted to three, and, at some, to two and a half days in the week.

This fall of wages commenced, it will be remarked, in 1815 and 1816; a period of depression in every branch of trade and commerce in the kingdom, and since which, none has regained its previous prosperity. It extended to every class of labourers; and the irritation and commotions to which it gave rise, are fresh in the minds of all. Many are the causes to which this universal depression has been attributed. At the time of its greatest pressure, it seemed to be the prevailing belief among the operatives, that it arose from excessive taxation. Taxation, however, has been scarcely perceptibly diminished, and the distress has passed away. Others have sought for this cause in the great political and commercial changes, attendant upon the transition, from war with almost the whole of Europe, to a state of universal peace; and to this, more than to any single cause, it seems to have been owing. Few, if any, at the period of its occurrence, thought of the restraints imposed by the combination laws; or of ascribing any of its effects to them. It may be true, that the operatives, in their efforts to escape from it, felt themselves shackled and confined by these enactments; but neither they, nor any one else, appear to have attributed to them any direct influence in its production. Such an idea seems to have had its origin at a much later period.

During the whole of this depression and attendant commotions, the Colliers, and we speak it to their credit, remained without a murmur, and without even demanding relief. Their wages had fallen greatly; but not, in general, we may safely say, to a greater extent than the reduction, at the same period, of the price of provisions. Notwithstanding, therefore, the fall of their wages, they were still able to earn enough to sustain themselves and their families.

Unattended, however, as this depression was, by any public manifestations of feeling on the part of the Colliers, it appears to have left an impression upon their minds, and created a strong desire of averting the recurrence of a similar evil. Actuated by these motives, they have been engaged, during the last two or three years, in devising means to accomplish this desired object; and, since the repeal of the laws against combinations, a plan for attaining it, by an organised and regulated association, or combination, among themselves, has been set on foot. Whether that plan be one of sound policy, or one, to which the public should submit in silence, is now the subject of consideration.

This scheme originated in the immediate neighbourhood of the city of Glasgow, the Scottish focus of organised systems of combination; and bears marks of the helping hand of others, who had preceded in the ranks of associated workmen. It has already been adopted by all the Colliers in Lanark, Renfrew, and Dumbarton, shires, the most populous part of Scotland; and much assiduity is, at present, directed towards establishing it in all the other coal districts of the kingdom.

The following is a copy of the original regulations of this combination, in so far as these have yet reached the public eye.

"Articles and Regulations for the Operative Colliers of Lanark, Dumbarton, and Renfrewshire.—Glasgow: Printed by Thomas Duncan, 159, Saltmarket. 1824.

We unite to obtain justice.
" Is not the labourer worthy of his hire? "

PREAMBLE.

As far as history, or experience, has taught us, every nation or people, having no common centre to act upon, but every man independent of the community at large, acts entirely for himself, on selfish principles, and without any given point or law, or even without natural judgment sufficient to discern the necessity of concentrating the judgment, experience, and abilities of such community, to protect them from becoming the easy prey of every ambitious or avaricious person, whose interest it may be to oppress them. Such nation or people have invariably become first the dupes, and then, of course, the slaves of any such men, who, by force or cunning, may have taken the advantage of the simplicity of their fellow-creatures, for the purpose of amassing immense property or fortune—solely realized from the wretchedly hard and laborious earnings of the poor. That this is the case with the Operative Colliers, at the present time, few will dare to deny. Ever disunited amongst themselves, they always have become an easy prey to those who have always studiously employed their every effort to keep open this fatal breach—even long and dear-bought experience has not been found sufficient to guard us against this fatal rock, that we have so often split upon, until reduced to the lowest ebb of human misery; and then, every effort for regaining that freedom and independence, so natural to Britons, was immediately paralysed by the iron grasp of that partial law, which enabled any tyrannical Master immediately to crush his fellow-subjects. That great obstacle being now abrogated, let the Operative Colliers contemplate with pleasure this piece of liberal policy, which has reinstated us in our rights as men, and, at the same time, enabled us to meet our Employers in the most fair and candid manner : therefore, let the Operative Body of Colliers bury in oblivion their past sufferings and jealousies, and, in one great body, unite themselves together; and, by so doing, they will defy every effort of those whose wish and interest it is to oppress them—let a well-understood and firm basis be formed, and firmly acted upon; and he, or they, that may wish to encroach upon this our rights and regulations, let the whole well-directed force of this our United Body be directed against he, or they, so offending, and continue so to act, until he, or they, again return within the proper limits. It is a thing as clear as daylight, that the wages of the Operative Colliers are reduced to an unprecedented degree of lowness; and, at what allowance the reducing system may stop, it is impossible to speculate upon. The reason why, the most superficial observer can easily discern, viz. the Operative, without any given point to act on, is wholly engrossed with the sordid principle of self, and almost always divided from the Body at large, while the Masters, by a well-regulated policy among themselves, take always the advantage of this want of union in the Operatives, and, consequently, lower their goods in the market, and, at the same time, with an unsparing hand, pull down the price of labour time after time; and where it may end, it is impossible to say, except they be, in a decisive manner, counteracted by the combined efforts of the Operative Body.

Deeply impressed with the truth, and conscious of the necessity of attending to what is recommended above, we, the Operative Colliers of Lanark, Dumbarton, and Renfrewshire, do hereby agree to associate ourselves, and to abide by the following Articles and Regulations:—

ARTICLE I.

Every Operative Collier to associate himself with the work that he is at present employed in, if such work be an associated body; and if it is not, with any other most answerable for himself, in Lanark, Dumbarton, and Renfrewshire.

ARTICLE II.

Every Operative to abide by, and conform himself to, all rules and regulations of such association as he may enter with, provided such rules and regulations are seen and approved of by our Preses and Committee, and sanctioned by a vote of the fair majority of its members.

ARTICLE III.

The interests of this private association shall be placed in the hands of a Preses and twelve Managers, chosen by votes from the body; but the general interests of the association shall be placed under the direction of a Committee of Delegates from the different works. Said Committee to meet weekly, for three months, after a general agreement, for to consider of such business as may be brought before them: and a General Committee to meet, at least once every six months, to be composed of the Preses, Treasurer, and Clerk of each private association, and as many of the Managers as may be found necessary, for the purpose of settling accounts with the General Committee.

ARTICLE IV.

If at any time it be found necessary, by the tyrannical measures of any Master, for any work to stop, such General Committee of Delegates to meet once a-week, for the purpose of advising and assisting such work, until it has its grievances properly and fairly redressed; or, if it be found advisable by said Committee, to find employment for said Operatives, as it is understood, that no Operative will be considered as liable to any claim on this association, if refusing to take employment in any work with his associated brethren; and no work to strike, or stop work, until advice be asked, and given by said Committee, after they have thoroughly considered the same: nor no man or work to enter into any litigation or suit at law, with his or their masters, until regular advice is asked, and given by said Committee, after they have thoroughly consulted and advised on the subject; and no suit at law to be entered into, except on account of a Master detaining of wages, or turning away a man without warning, and unsettled with, or refusing to pay, on account of not working on a broken price.

ARTICLE V.

But any man, or men, being thrown idle, by refusing to work under the stated wages of said Committee, to be allowed ten shillings per week, until their grievances be redressed, or by themselves, or by the Committee, find employment. No man to receive any aliment for being idle for one week; but, if he continue so for two weeks, to be paid at the end of the second week, and also be regularly paid for each week, for the whole period of his, or their, idleness, unless he, or they, refuse to work, after work has been procured.

ARTICLE VI.

No member to receive any aliment, until he brings a sufficient line from the Preses, and, at least, two of the Managers of the association that he may belong to, specifying the justness of his claims, and defining the reasons, in a clear and proper manner. Such lines to be inspected and looked into, before a General Committee, as soon as possible; and, if a work, to receive no support until the regularity of their proceedings is ascertained, as specified in Article V.

ARTICLE VII.

Every man or men, so conforming, shall receive, after the specified period, as in Article V, the sum of ten shillings per week, from the Treasurer of his or their association. Each association to bear an equal proportion according to the number of their members, and remit regularly, when desired, such sums as may be required, to the General Committee of Delegates, for the purpose of distribution.

ARTICLE VIII.

Each work to have its own association, and to retain its own monies, as it of itself may think most proper; no other work or committee having any cognizance, in any manner of way, with any separate association, farther than of seeing the regular payments made, when required, according to the number of its associated members.

ARTICLE IX.

Every Operative, having entered said association, is to continue to pay sixpence each fourteen days, for three months from the present date hereof, and, after that period, whatever may be agreed upon by a committee of delegates assembled; and to be paid in such place as may be intimated by their Officer, at least twenty-four hours before payment. Every member who neglects to pay for two succeeding payments, shall be fined in one penny on the third payment; that is, by neglecting, for six weeks, to pay his regular payments, to be fined in one penny, and an additional penny every succeeding fourteen days, till

H

the expiration of three months; when, if still deficient of settling his accounts by payment, to receive forty-eight hours regular warning, and, if continuing still refractory, and not paying up said payments and fines, his name to be erased from the books, except an admissible excuse is given to the Preses and Managers of said association.

ARTICLE X.

Any Operative Collier, residing within the boundary of the association, who may wish to enter said association, by paying up all payments and dues of the same, will be admitted till the 16th October, 1824; and, from this date, to pay one pound as entry-money, until 16th November, when the entry-money shall be two pounds until 30th November, and from that date, no person to be admitted under the sum of five pounds—and to conform to all rules and regulations of the association.

ARTICLE XI.

Any person having left the coal-trade, and following another occupation, but wishing to join this association, shall pay, as entry-money, the following sums, viz. Any person, having left the trade three months preceding 27th September, shall pay the sum of two pounds; and any person, that has been six months from the trade, to pay the sum of three pounds; if nine months, to pay the sum of four pounds; and, if one year, to pay the sum of five pounds; before being admitted a member of the association.

ARTICLE XII.

Every associated man, being the father of a family, shall be at liberty to employ his sons as he may think for his own advantage, according to the rules of said association; but he shall receive no rights for them until they are ten years of age, and he shall then receive one-fourth of a man's work for a boy, until he arrives at the age of thirteen, and he shall then receive one-half of a man's right, and continue so to work, until he arrives at fifteen, when he shall receive three-fourths of a man's right, until he arrives at seventeen years of age, when, by giving one month's notice, he shall receive a man's full right. Every boy, on receiving one-fourth, to pay one shilling; one-half, one shilling and sixpence; three-fourths, two shillings; and a man's full right, two shillings and sixpence.

ARTICLE XIII.

Any boy, being the son of an Operative Collier associated, and his father being dead or disabled, or otherwise employed, shall receive the same benefits as are in Article XII. But any boy, not being the son of an Operative, shall receive and pay as follows: At thirteen years of age, he shall receive one-fourth of a man's right; and at sixteen, one-half of a man's right; and at eighteen, three-fourths; and at twenty, he shall receive a man's full right, by giving one month's regular notice. Said boy to pay as follows: On receiving one-fourth, to pay one pound; and one-half, to pay two pounds; three-fourths, to pay three pounds; and, on receiving a man's full right, to pay two pounds, making, in whole, five pounds; and to find sufficient security, by giving two men more, to the satisfaction of the work. The Operative who he may be employed with, to come good for all and the whole of said money, and its regular payments.

ARTICLE XIV.

Every man, not being an Operative, and wishing to learn the same, shall receive and pay as follows: that is, he shall pay five pounds sterling, and serve three years, by way of apprenticeship. Two pounds ten shillings to be paid upon entry, and the remaining two pounds ten shillings to be paid by regular instalments, of ten shillings the first year, and one pound each succeeding year; and he shall receive one-half of a man's right the first year, and three-fourths of a man's right the two succeeding years; when, at the expiration of said three years, he shall become a full man. No associated Operative shall take any man to draw or work with him, or employ him at coalworking, or any thing connected therewith, unless strictly conforming to said Article.

ARTICLE XV.

No Operative beyond the boundaries of this association to be admitted into it, unless he may have associated, given his Master the regular warning, dropped work, and stood firm with the body for at least six weeks, for an advance of wages; otherwise, to be admitted on the terms specified in Article XIV.

ARTICLE XVI.

Every Operative shall, on any business taking place, hear a full and clear discussion of the subject;

when, after a vote is taken, the majority to decide, although contrary to his opinion—and he must abide by, and conform to, the same, equally the same as if it had been his own vote or opinion.

ARTICLE XVII.

Should any dispute take place betwixt any of the different associations, the dispute to be submitted to the general meeting of delegates, whose decision is final.

ARTICLE XVIII.

At a general meeting of delegates, they shall have it in their power to alter, amend, or erase, provided proper notice is given to each work or association fourteen days previous; and they shall have it in their power to make new articles, provided it be found necessary by two-thirds of the members present: but no vote or procedure shall have power to interfere with each association keeping, under its own charge, its own cash, or monies, and their keeping it in any way that to them may seem most eligible.

ARTICLE XIX.

Every associated member, upon leaving the present work where he is employed, must receive a ticket, signed by the Preses of his association; this ticket he is to give to the Preses of the association where he may enter. The ticket to signify whether the member be clear, and, if deficient in payment, to pay an equal sum to the new society: and the said ticket shall likewise specify how much may be due to said Operative by said old association. This ticket to be given to the Treasurer of the new association, where, if any emergency may occur, the said new Treasurer may return this ticket, and receive the amount of cash due on said ticket, as soon as convenient after date of the said ticket.

ARTICLE XX.

Every associated member who may have allowed himself to fall back in the association, and, according to Article IX, be erased from the same, he shall, upon application to the Preses and Committee, be again admitted, upon paying up all and the whole of his payments, and expenses that may have occurred during the time of his absenting himself from said association.

ARTICLE XXI.

Every associated member, upon leaving his present work, and going to another, shall pay an entry of two shillings—to be paid by instalments of sixpence every fourteen days, and booked in the books of said association. All entries and fines to be paid into the association, and booked, as aforesaid.

ARTICLE XXII.

No Operative, being a member of this association, shall be at liberty to engage himself with any Master for any given time, or at any given price; or, receiving money on loan, shall not be allowed to bind himself to pay the same at so much per cart, but, upon fourteen days notice being given, and the money being paid, shall have liberty to depart from the work.

ARTICLE XXIII.

That no motion made at any meeting of delegates shall be acted upon presently, but must lie over till next meeting, when every motion is to be brought forward in its due order.

FINIS."

———

WHAT a contrast between the present condition of the Colliers, and that in which they were found by the Act of 1775, do the spirit and principles of these regulations manifest! Nay, what a striking revolution must have taken place in their state, and in the sentiments of this nation, since 1799! Then, we found an attempt made—an attempt which, but for the opposition, not of the Colliers themselves, but of the friends to them and to freedom and liberality, seemed to promise to be successful—to reduce the Colliers to a state of bondage to their Masters. Here, we see the Colliers proposing, by their own unaided powers, to lord it over these Masters, and shackle and constrain them in the use and enjoyment of their property, to almost as great a degree as the Masters proposed to inthral them.

In the preamble, there is explicitly stated, as the cause of the combination, the opinion which has been already noticed, that the depression of wages has been occasioned by advantages afforded to the Masters, by the combination laws. This bears upon its face the marks of improbability, nay, of impracticability, when the state of this country is, for a moment, considered; and is not borne out by a single fact in the history of the collieries. The present may well be termed the age of commercial and manufacturing competition; and competition and combination are as opposed as light and darkness. Granting, that the Master Colliers wished to combine to bear down the wages of the workmen, it would require but small penetration in them to perceive, that such a combination could be prejudicial only to themselves. For, what would be its effect? If the wages of the Colliers were diminished below the fair remuneration for their services, corresponding to the wages of other labourers, the certain effect would be, to drive them to seek other employments; and thus, to occasion a scarcity of hands in the coal-trade. If the Masters still persevered, and carried on their works with fewer hands, the produce of these works must be lessened; and, consequently, the profit of the Master, and the return for his capital, not so great as before he entered into the combination. But, in this last, we are supposing a case which never has occurred, and, we may safely say, never will occur. The invariable effect of a scarcity of hands, in any branch of trade, is an increase of wages to the labourers in that trade. So long, therefore, as competition remains, and our workmen are left to the freedom of choosing their trade and their Master, their wages must find their fair and proper level.

But, even were it not so ; were the principle which has given rise to this association well founded; the spirit, and the tendency, of its regulations are not warranted by such premises, and are inconsistent with the prosperity of the country. Much is said, in their preamble, of the selfishness of individuals; but the selfishness of an individual is insignificant and contemptible in its consequences, compared with that of a powerful association. Here is a system of articles, whose very essence is selfishness; which tells to the world, that the Colliers are determined, if they can, cost what it will to their fellow-countrymen—impair as it may their comforts, or injure the commerce and manufactures of the nation—to enjoy whatever degree of ease and comfort they may choose to consider their due.

Such ease and comfort, the association proposes to attain, by means of the wages to be paid to its members; and, accordingly, the aim of the regulations is, to put it in their power to determine the price to be paid by the Masters for their labour. To obtain this power, it was necessary, that the association should monopolise the trade of coal-hewing; and so restrict the number of workmen, that the supply of coal should always bear a certain proportion to the demand. There is not, in the whole of the regulations yet published, any thing which expressly says, that the members of the association alone shall be permitted to work as Colliers. Such an open avowal would have been illegal, and subjected the association to immediate prosecution. On that account, alone, we may say, has it been omitted; for,

the spirit of the regulations promulgated is such, as
to leave not the slightest shadow of doubt, that the
understanding and determination of the whole members of the association are, that no unassociated person shall be allowed to work with them. What,
otherwise, would be the use of the regulations regarding apprentices and returning Colliers? Would
any man pay a fee, and labour, at an under wage,
for three or seven years, if he could obtain the same
benefits without these preliminaries? Without such
an understanding, and without a firm determination invariably to act up to it, the association, and
all its rules, were a mere mockery. Of the spirit,
with which this understood law will be enforced,
we may see some indication in the preamble to
the Rules. There, the Operative Body of Colliers
are called upon to unite themselves together, and
defy every effort of those whose wish and interest it
is to oppress them: to let a well *understood* and firm
basis be formed and *acted upon;* and the whole well-
directed force of their united body be directed against
him, or them, who may encroach upon their rights
and regulations; and continue so to act, until the
offenders return within their proper limits. But, we
are not left to inference and conjecture, merely, on
this point: the Colliers have, already, *acted* upon this
understood law. It is a fact, well known by every
person connected with the collieries, that no individual Collier will agree to enter into a coal-work,
against the voice of the general body of workmen;
and no man has yet been found, so resolute, as to
bear up against the molestations which are practised,
for compelling an unwelcome stranger to abandon

the work. These means of molestation are well known to the masters; but are easily practised by the Colliers, during their hours of labour, when the regular superintendence, which accompanies all other kinds of labour, cannot be conveniently exercised.

The regulations to restrict the number of workmen are sufficiently explicit. The sons of members of the association are not to be permitted to receive a man's wages, till the age of seventeen, and payment of seven shillings; and no other person can now be admitted a member, except on payment of five pounds; and, besides, a boy, who is not the son of an Operative, must serve an apprenticeship of seven years; and a person of seventeen years of age or upwards, an apprenticeship of three years.

The impolicy of such regulations, and the injury which must be done to the community by enforcing them, are manifest. The free use and circulation of labour will be obstructed; and the wages of the Colliers forced up to an unnatural rate. The Masters will be excluded from the free enjoyment of their property, and so trammelled in the disposal of the produce of their works, that all competition among them must cease. And the workmen will attain the complete control of the supply of the coal-market; and, consequently, the power of regulating the price at which that commodity shall be sold to the public. The association is, indeed, a combination of the Colliers to defraud the public.

The advantages of a free circulation of labour, and an unfettered competition among traders, have been so often, and so fully, illustrated by our ablest writers on political economy, that to dwell on them here would be superfluous. That the regulations of the Colliers must have the tendency, in these respects, which we have attributed to them, seems too evident to require explanation. The avowed intention of their framers is, to obtain, by means of them, an increase of wages, and to prevent the Masters from affecting, by competition, the price of coal; and the means proposed, for accomplishing these objects, are, the exclusion of other labourers from the occupation of a Collier, in all its branches. The trade of a Collier, if trade it can be called, is one of such easy acquirement, that it requires no preparatory initiation. Any workman in the country is equal to its performance, and able to become, in a short time, as expert as the most thorough-bred Collier. But, the simpler any occupation is, and the more easily it can be acquired, the more injurious do restrictions, upon the freedom of entering into it, become. In no case, therefore, can they be more hurtful than in that of the Colliers. The effects of the exclusive privileges of corporations of craftsmen within burghs, how much soever these have been deprecated, and the unsoundness of their policy exposed, may be termed harmless, when compared with the consequences which would flow from the exercise of the same privileges by common labourers: yet, such the Colliers are; and the privileges, which they would arrogate to themselves, are as exclusive as those of a corporation of craftsmen.

There are other peculiarities in these regulations, which render them of a character still more injurious. Hitherto, the privileges of corporations, and the restrictions upon trade and commerce, have flowed from the Legislature and Government of the country. They have all been devised by a power, which professed, at least, to confer no benefit, and impose no restriction, by which the interests of the community should be made to suffer. They can, too, be enforced only by the constituted authorities of the land, and are subject to the constant check and control of an enlightened Government. In the regulations of the Colliers, however, we behold a system of rules, meant to have all the force of charters of corporations or legislative enactments, formed by the men who are to benefit by them, and by whom the observance of them is to be enforced. The Colliers, along with many other trades, seem to have formed the idea, that Parliament, by the repeal of the laws against combinations, has had it in view to encourage the formation of associations; and devolved the power of legislation upon the Committees of the Operatives, for the purpose of framing laws for the new establishments. Instead of regarding this repeal as the evidence of a liberal policy, and a tribute to the increased knowledge of the working classes—a tribute, paid from a belief that these had now attained an extent of information and improvement of character, which rendered any peculiar superintendence of their conduct unnecessary; and would sufficiently restrain, without the aid of statutes, from actions injurious to the prosperity of the country—each association seems to have looked upon this repeal as the signal of a

license to be revenged upon the Masters, for ills
which it imagined had been inflicted by them on its
trade; and to oppress, in its turn; and aggrandise its
members, at the expense of the prosperity of the
country. There is one peculiarity of the regulations
of the Colliers very apparent; and which strikingly
marks their origin from the novel legislating power
of which we have just spoken. In legal corporations,
the fees and emoluments of apprenticeships go to the
Masters, by means of whose capital, the work is carried on. Not so with the Colliers. All these fees
and emoluments are to go to the Colliers themselves
—to servants, who derive their own employment
from the capital of the Masters. What is the language of this peculiarity, and, indeed, of the whole
articles? It is, that the Colliers look upon the collieries as their own, and not the property of the Masters, and will rule and manage these accordingly.
Nor, here, are we left to inference alone. It is a fact,
of which every Coal-proprietor and Coalmaster is
perfectly aware, that the present race of Colliers
already consider the mines to be as much the property of the workmen, as of the Masters, at whose
risk, and with whose capital, they have been established, and are carried on.

But the effect of these regulations, of the most importance to the public—the one, at least, most likely
to come home to their feelings—is, that the Colliers
will, thereby, attain the complete control of the coal-
market, and the power of fixing the price of coal.
This effect naturally results from the exaction of a
fee, and the serving of an apprenticeship, previously

to being allowed to work as a Collier. One of two things must follow from these restrictions; either the number of Colliers, and, consequently, the supply of coal, will be diminished; or, the wages of the Colliers will attain a height, sufficient to compensate, not only for the daily toil and danger of the workman, but, also, for the burdens and exactions to which he has been subjected by the rules of the association. In either case, there must follow a rise in the wages of the Colliers, and in the price of coal. These causes have not yet had time to operate; when they have begun to do so, they will render a high rate of wage permanent. Yet, even without their direct aid, and merely by dint of the union among themselves established by their regulations, and by striking work, the Colliers have already succeeded in raising their wages considerably; and increased the price of coals to the consumers nearly one hundred per cent. That any body of men should have the power of regulating the price of an article of manufacture, is injurious—of an article of natural produce, most pernicious. We deprecate the exercise of such a power, even when guided by all the wisdom of the Legislature. How vigorously, then, ought we to exert ourselves to crush it, when exercised by a body of men for their own benefit; and these, too, men of scanty information and narrow views. Yet, this has been done by the Colliers. When done by Government, we submit; of two evils, choosing the least: but shall we submit to the latter? We cry out against the corn laws, and against restrictions upon trade and commerce; but the Colliers have entered into a combination against the community at large, by which, the price of a necessary of life has been augmented, in a greater proportion, than the price of bread by the corn laws, even in the opinion of their most vehement opponents. The Colliers have imposed a burden upon our manufactures, more grievous by far than many of those imposed by Government; and, strange to say, not a single voice seems raised against them!

The regulations of the Colliers must operate as a direct tax upon the national industry. This is always the consequence where the free circulation of labour is obstructed, and the cost of producing any article elevated by factitious means. The public are, thereby, charged for the article more than its proper value, proportioned to other articles of produce or manufacture. This effect, in an article of luxury or of mere comfort, would speedily be counteracted by a falling off. or entire cessation, of the demand. But coal, in this climate, is a necessary of life, and essential to almost every branch of manufactures. It must be had at whatever price it can. A rise of price will, no doubt, diminish the demand, but the diminution will be made at the expense of the comfort of the inhabitants, and prosperity of the manufactures of the country. This diminution, however, can never go beyond a certain extent; and the Colliers, by diminishing the number of workmen, have the power of counteracting its effect in producing a fall in their wages. To prevent this effect from the recent rise, they have limited their work and the output of coal, so as barely to meet the daily demand, and prevent the accumulation of a stock by the Masters. The

Corn Laws, as they at present stand, have been regarded as an oppression; how much more grievous would it have been, to have had the price of grain raised, by a combination of all the landlords and farmers of the country, to any extent which they chose to think a sufficient remuneration to themselves? The combination of the Colliers is of a kind like this, but much more effectual to accomplish its object. Corn is grown every where, and can be cheaply and plentifully imported; but not so coal. The want of coal, or the necessity of importing it, would be the ruin of the country. There is thus left no check over the Colliers, as there would be over the farmers.

A rise in the price of coals must also operate as a grievous tax upon every branch of manufacture, and consequently of commerce; and as a direct tax upon every inhabitant of this country, but more especially grievous upon the poor, who are the great consumers of this article, as of every other of prime necessity. Other taxes are sufficiently heavy; but these go to support the general expenditure of the nation. They are made, also, to fall as lightly as possible upon the poor; and none directly affect the necessaries of life in their state of raw produce. But this tax, imposed by the Colliers, is to go into their private pockets, and to form a fund to enable them the more effectually to continue its imposition. It is to fall, too, on an article of raw produce indispensible to many manufactures, and so shackle them throughout all their processes. And it is to fall upon a necessary of life, and weigh indiscriminately on the poor and the rich.

But for the mildness of the present winter, it might have reduced many of the poor to starvation, or caused commotions and riots of a most injurious kind.

The effect of a struggle, on the part of the workmen, to increase their wages, is thus described in a very recent publication, conducted with eminent ability: " The workman struggles with all his strength, to get " his wages increased; the manufacturer and mer- " chant, in like manner, to get their profits increased. " As the total sale diminishes, it is necessary for their " subsistence that they obtain more for each separate " article. Their joint efforts soon succeed in raising " the price of all goods, coming from their hands, " but *especially goods of prime necessity, because the* " *sellers of these give the law to buyers who cannot do* " *without such goods.* A rise in the price of these " commodities re-acts anew on wages and profits; the " disorganisation becomes complete; national pro- " ductions cost much higher than those of countries " not oppressed by a similar system. They cannot " support a competition in foreign markets; expor- " tation ceases; demand is not renewed; and the " nation sinks under a frightful distress." Similar must be the effects of any system, which raises the price of an article, so necessary to the comforts of the inhabitants, and so indispensible to the manufactures of the country, as coal. Its price must regulate, in a considerable degree, the price of every thing to whose produce it is subservient; and, from a forced and sustained rise of that price, must follow the same frightful distress traced by the writer from whom we have just quoted.

But of all the labourers in the kingdom, Colliers have the least occasion to complain of their wages, or seek, by unnatural means, to force their rise. The labour of a Collier is performed under so many privations, inconveniences, and dangers, that his daily wages must always be far greater than those of any other labourer of the same rank. The Collier may, indeed, be regarded as a common labourer to whom a premium is given, for engaging in a hazardous occupation. This premium must always amount to something; and to its amount must his wages exceed those of other common labourers. Accordingly we have seen, that, during the late period of manufacturing distress, and when the weavers and common labourers were reduced to beggary, the Colliers enjoyed wages which the others would have considered most comfortable, and which so supplied their wants, that they submitted without murmur. Had their wages been as low as those of many other classes, and as insufficient for procuring the necessaries of life, the Colliers are not of a character more likely to have submitted to them in silence, than the others.

We have already said, that, even granting that the depression of wages had been owing to the facility of associating together, afforded to the masters, but denied to the workmen, by the laws against combinations, the regulations of the Colliers are unwarranted by such premisses; and overshoot the aim which, on such a principle, they ought to have had in view. These regulations are more than sufficient to counteract the injurious effects of any association among the Masters. To accomplish this, it was only necessary,

that the Colliers bound themselves in a body not to
work below a stipulated wage. If that wage was a
proper one, and proportioned to the price paid for
other labour throughout the county, they must have
succeeded in obtaining it. Every species of labour,
when left to perfect freedom, must find its fair level.
The only possible mode, in which the combination
laws could operate to restrain this freedom, was,
by allowing an union of effort upon the part of the
masters, and not of the workmen. The moment,
which gave to the Colliers the power of uniting and
opposing their collective efforts to the Masters, dissolved the power of the latter, and banished every
restraint upon the freedom of the Collier's labour.
Previously to the repeal of these laws, the united
power of the masters was opposed to the divided
efforts of the workmen; the object of the repeal was,
to permit the full energies of the latter to come into
action, and to place masters and men on equal ground.
The efforts of the Colliers ought, then, to have been
directed solely against their Masters. This alone
should be the object of their system of Articles; as
this alone is warranted by the principle, upon which
these Articles profess to be founded. Instead of this,
however, these Articles are directed, not so much
against the masters, as against the public. The spirit
of them indeed is, that the collieries are the property
of the workmen, and to be subject to their control;
but the use, which they hold out as to be made of
these collieries, is to operate to the prejudice of the
public, to the impairing of our comforts, and the injury of our manufactures. If the profits of the Coalmaster are not diminished, it is a matter of indifference

to him whether the produce of his work be great or small; its price, high or low. It is undoubtedly true, that a forced rise in the price of coal will, in the end, operate to the prejudice of the lessees or proprietors of the coal. But this is not its direct and immediate effect. That is, to injure manufactures and encroach on the comforts of the people. Accordingly, we see that many of the Coalmasters are lukewarm and indifferent, when applied to for their aid to put down the association; and refuse to co-operate with their more liberal and enlightened brethren. Many of them are, at present, by the recent rise on the price of coal caused by the association, pocketing larger gains than before, and cannot, or will not, see the ultimate ruinous consequences to themselves.

It would seem as if the repeal of the laws against combinations, had turned the brains of our workmen; and, in the consequent state of hallucination, they seem to have imagined, that by these laws had been caused all their former privations and distresses, and that to elevate them to comfort and happiness for the time to come, nothing more was necessary but to combine and associate together; as if the associating of workmen could create a market for the produce of their labour, to any extent, and at any price, which they chose to determine. These laws have existed long, and their effect on the condition of the workmen, had, long before their repeal, become in almost every case merely nominal. In theory, they might be regarded as restraints upon labour; but, in practice, they had long ceased to be so. The wages of our labourers were as high before their repeal, as they would have been had they never existed. But it seems to have been too much for the belief of the workmen, that the repeal of laws, even so inoperative, should not be attended with some great and palpable change upon themselves. No sooner therefore was the repeal made, than they sought to realise this change; and hence, the spirit of combination which has since been manifested;—hence, the numerous associations of the workmen;—and hence, the straining after unnatural improvements in their condition; and the overstepping the limits of prudence and sound policy in their systems of regulations. To check the effects of these regulations, founded in error and want of information, and of a most injurious tendency, is the duty of all.

Many of the Coalmasters have professed to look upon the association of their workmen with indifference, and as likely soon to fall to pieces of itself. But does its short history exhibit any mark of such a character? No. We have seen the Operative Cotton-spinners unite against their Masters; and the association broken by the latter, after a long and vigorous struggle. But have we seen the Coalmasters unite against the Colliers? No. We have seen the reverse; we have seen them succumb to all the unreasonable regulations and demands of their workmen. The association of the Operative Spinners was opposed, at its very commencement, and before its funds had accumulated; and yet, how powerful was the resistance which it made. The association of the Colliers has, at its very birth, been victorious over the Masters, and will it be more easily put down, or more likely to fall asunder, when its funds have grown, and the bonds of its union been consolidated by long continuance? Of all trades, the Colliers possess the greatest facilities for associating together; and are placed in circumstances, the most apt to promote strength and intimacy of coalition. Isolated, in a manner, during their labour, from all society with men of other occupations; and dwelling, in bodies by themselves, around the pits, the Colliers of each work form as it were one family. They are removed, during the greatest part of their time, from the superintendance of their Masters; and may concert their measures together without fear of interference or disturbance. If too, they will exclude the introduction of unassociated workmen among them, how much more easily and effectually can this be done, where a coal-pit is the scene of labour, than where this is a mill or any place above ground? When the Cotton-spinners struck work, the mills, notwithstanding all the exertions of the Masters to introduce new hands, remained shut and unemployed for upwards of three months. This strike was confined to Lanarkshire alone, and cotton-yarn is easily transported from one district to another; yet its effects were injurious. How ruinous must they have been, had it extended over the whole kingdom. If the Colliers, therefore, were to strike work, and the Masters make as vigorous an effort to put them down, as was made against the Cotton-spinners, the coal-works might, notwithstanding, remain long idle. Were this to take place in Lanarkshire alone, it would be productive of most serious consequences. But, when it is considered that all the Colliers in Lanark, Renfrew, and Dum-

barton, shires, are banded together; that, ere such a
strike take place, the whole Colliers in Scotland may
have joined the association; that the funds to support
the strike must have increased, far beyond those pos-
sessed by the Cotton-spinners; and that coal, even if
it were to be had, beyond the boundaries of these
three shires, for the period of the strike, can be transported only at a great expense; how dreadful must
be the consequences of such a stoppage of the coal-
works. It would paralyse every branch of trade and
commerce; shut every manufactory; and throw all
their workmen idle. As coal, too, is a necessary of
life, it would subject every class of society to the most
intolerable privation and suffering. Even were the
old Colliers, ere such frightful effects had taken place,
withdrawn from the collieries, and new labourers
introduced and protected by force of arms (for this
would indeed be necessary), some time would elapse
before such a measure could be resorted to,—witness
the continuance of the last strike;—and these new
workers thus commencing their labours, when coals
were in immediate and extraordinary requisition, and
ignorant of the nature of the work, must, to meet in
any degree the demand, be provided in such numbers,
as to disturb most injuriously the occupations whence
they were taken. In all cases as yet, the workers
who had struck have gained, and therefore we are
warranted in saying, that, in future cases, these workers will gain their object, before such an introduction
of new hands. In every case, the price of the commodity will be augmented; and the injury to the
country will be great.

We call, therefore, upon the Coal-owners, as they value their own interest; on the Coalmasters, as they value their interest and the liberty of employing their capital, to join in breaking the association of the Colliers,—in expelling from its Articles, every thing which is noxious and hurtful in its tendency. Let the Colliers, and we most heartily join in wishing that they may, enjoy a full and liberal remuneration for their dangerous and laborious toils; but let them not have the power of arbitrarily and forcibly fixing a remuneration for themselves. Let them have the freedom, in its fullest extent, of checking every species and degree of oppression; but let them not have the power of oppressing.

In 1799, we have seen the Public petitioning, and the Parliament interposing, to have the Colliers protected against the encroachments of their Masters on their liberty; we call, therefore, upon the Public to petition, and the Parliament to interfere, in 1825, to protect the Coalmasters and the Coal Trade, from the encroachments and thrall of the Colliers. The Public petitioned, in 1799, from a regard to the liberty of every class of the subjects of this kingdom; we call upon them to petition now, from a regard to the same liberty, and as they value their own comfort, and the prosperity of our land. The Parliament legislated, in 1799, to prevent the oppression of one class of men; let them now legislate to prevent the oppression of many classes. We deprecate, as much as the Colliers or any class of operatives can do, the revival of the old Combination Laws. We rejoiced at their repeal, because we considered their existence in the

Statute-book as a blot on the liberality of the age; and we hope yet to see the freedom from control, which that repeal has conferred, soberly and rationally enjoyed by the industrious workmen of this land. But we would, that every class in this country should enjoy the same freedom in the control and disposal of its property, as the workmen have attained of their labour. We would, that no class be allowed in any way, either by partial enactments of the Legislature, or by organised associations, to have the power of coercing and oppressing another. And we call upon the Public, and the Parliament, to limit and restrain the associations of the Colliers from the exercise of such a power.

JAMES HEDDERWICK AND SON, PRINTERS, GLASGOW.

COPY OF A LETTER

FROM JOSEPH HUME, Esq. M. P. TO Mr. JOHN ALLAN, SHIPWRIGHT, DUNDEE.

London, March 26th, 1825.

SIR,

In answer to your letter of the 17th instant, I have to state, that the proposition which you submit, of interfering with the Master Shipwrights, as to the number of years during which they should bind apprentices, would be contrary to the principle on which the Government is now acting, of leaving every man to conduct his own business in the manner which he shall think best, provided it is not injurious to the community.

It was on that principle, that the combination laws were repealed, and the workmen left at liberty to sell their labour, and employ their time, as they might think most to their advantage. It was on that principle also, that the act of Elizabeth, which required every person learning a trade, to serve an apprenticeship of three, five, or seven years, was repealed.

The application which you wish to make to Parliament, is directly opposed to these important changes; and I cannot but express my surprise, that the operative shipwrights of Dundee, should so far forget themselves, as (while they are at perfect liberty to do as they please,) to propose to interfere with that freedom, to which the masters are entitled as well as the men.

I have farther to say, that if the plan proposed, respecting apprentices at Dundee, and other places, were carried into effect, it would not produce the results which the operatives anticipate; and I am quite certain, that if the operatives in every part of the country, do not act with more fairness, moderation, and prudence than they are now doing, the Legislature will be obliged to retrace their steps, and to adopt measures to check the unreasonable proceedings and exorbitant demands, made on the commerce of the country, by the unions of seamen, shipwrights, and other trades, too often accompanied with violence.

With an anxious desire to see the operatives fully rewarded for their labour, I must intreat the operative shipwrights not to interfere with their masters, or to take any steps that may lead to the alternative, which I have pointed out as probable.

I remain,

SIR,

Your obedient Servant,

(Signed)   JOSEPH HUME.

1825

OBSERVATIONS

ON

Mr. HUSKISSON's SPEECH

ON

THE LAWS

RELATING TO

Combinations of Workmen.

———————

J. Innes, Printer, 61, *Wells-st. Oxford-st. London.*

IN the last session, the Parliament, ~~with much credit to itself,~~ *unanimously* repealed all the laws which forbid workmen to combine to raise their wages, or to regulate the hours of working. The measure was a wise one : it has already caused a considerable improvement among the working people—has, to a great extent, removed the evils which the laws it repealed had produced—has put an end to the enormous cruelties, which those laws gave bad men the power to inflict, and to the practice of cruelty, which under those laws was frequently inflicted on workmen. In a vast many instances such an approximation towards a good understanding between workmen and their employers has been made, as bids fair to extinguish for ever those feelings of suspicion, jealousy, and hatred, which kept the masters and workmen more or less in a state of hostility, debased the people, and made them worse members of society than but for these laws they would have been. The barbarous way in which the laws were frequently applied and the constant apprehension that even, for the most meritorious conduct, these acts might be resorted to, had separated the two classes of masters and workmen so completely, had made them so universally enemies, ~~as to make it~~ doubtful ~~with many~~ whether or not they could be reconciled. Yet the repeal of these partial, unjust and cruel laws has already done much towards effecting this desirable purpose, and ~~will~~, if our legislators have a little patience, ^produce a state of things which, *will* when compared with the former state of things, will both deserve and receive the approbation of every man, .who has not from feelings of pride, or from such an inordinate desire of gain as overpowers all benevolent feelings, become indifferent to the welfare of the great body of the people, careless whether they become respectable in their demeanour, decent in their persons, and well-instructed in their duties, or be put back into a state of ignorance and barbarism. *be suffered to remain*

~~Let~~ the law ^remain as it is for but two or three years, ~~and~~ such a progress will be made towards all that is desirable in the state of the working people, that it will be ~~quite~~ impossible for any one to doubt the wisdom of that Parliament, which repealed the laws against combinations. To. the advocates for the re-enactment of the laws or any modification of them, it may be observed, that now, when education has made great strides and is rapidly becoming universal, when ^institutions *″* are ~~being~~ established in most of the principal towns in the kingdom, for teaching the working people, not only what, as to them, was formerly called education, namely, to spell a sentence and scrawl their names, but to instruct them, in trade, art, and science, and in moral duties, it is quite impossible for them to retrograde in knowledge; they can never again sink on the scale of society—they can never again be classed promiscuously with the dissolute and abandoned. A separation has ~~already~~ commenced, and those who will neither learn, nor practice the duties of good citizens, will soon be discarded and become a distinct grade, equally the contempt of the well-informed working people, and of those whose circumstances place them higher on the scale of society. The impulse has been given, it has been and continues to be accelerated, it ~~can~~ can never more be stayed. In such a state of society, with such certain prospects of improvement, either the law must accord with the state of the people, or the people will despise ~~the law, and those~~ law makers, ~~which and~~ ~~who they see and feel, are too barbarous, and~~ too ignorant, or too careless of the absurdities they commit, and the evils they heap upon those, whose intelligence and moral worth fairly intitle them to treatment directly the reverse.

Bad laws make bad subjects; bad laws when applied to an enlightened community, must always produce injurious consequences. Re-enact the recently repealed laws against workmen, and similar effects will be produced to those which bad laws have produced in Ireland, with this difference, that the same sense of oppression, the same hatred both of their employers and of the Government itself; the same desire of revenge will be directed, not by uncombined ignorance, but by a combination of intelligence, such as has never before been seen. Surely the Legislature will pause, will look at the actual condition of society, will compare it with its former state, and will not absurdly sanction proposals which can do no good whatever, but which on the contrary cannot fail to do great mischief to the whole community.

On the 29th March Mr. Huskisson moved for, and obtained a Select Committee, " to inquire into the effects " of the Act 5 Geo. IV. c. 95, in respect to the conduct " of workmen and others, in different parts of the United " Kingdom ; and to report their opinion, how far it may " may be necessary to repeal or amend the said act." Mr. Huskisson, in his speech which preceded his motion for the Committee, took, as the newspapers report, the part of the masters only, and omitted to say one word in favour of the men. Many representations had, he said, been made to him, and still more to Mr. Peel, of the bad conduct of the men, and no doubt this was true—true as to numbers of masters complaining—true also in some instances as to the bad conduct of the men. But Mr. Huskisson did not tell the House, as he might have done, that he and his colleague had also received many representations from the men, of the bad conduct of the masters. He did not tell the House that he, as well as other ministers, had received the thanks of large bodies of workmen ; that those thanks were accompanied with the strongest expressions of gratitude for the benefits which

had been so justly conferred upon them, and with decla-
rations of the most determined resolution, not only to
obey the law themselves, but to discountenance in others
every act which had a contrary tendency, as well as every
kind of conduct calculated to revive, or to continue, the
suspicion and want of confidence which the laws against
combinations had engendered or perpetuated. Mr. Huskisson did not say, he had been informed that in many
places where the greatest hatred and discontent had prevailed, and the most rancorous hostility had been carried
on, peace and good will had once more been restored.
Yet all this, and much more than this he might have said,
and ought to have said. He took a partial view of the
case. Instead of a comprehensive, statesmanlike view,
he became the advocate of the strongest party against the
weakest, and was so unwise as to threaten the people with
all but " *a vigour beyond the law*," although in other
parts of his speech he admitted that the law, as it stood,
without any straining, was fully equal to the prevention
or correction of every real evil. Mr. Peel was still more
determined in his hostility ; but of Mr. Peel, in such
matters as these, nothing need be said. One is, however,
grieved to see a man like Mr. Huskisson lending himself,
as on this occasion he has lent himself ; pulling down his
own reputation for knowledge, involving himself unnecessarily in difficulties, agitating and torturing, with appre-
hensions of terrible evils, a large portion of the community,

when this portion is generally disposed, not only to be peaceable, but desirous to prevent future disputes by putting an end to long continued animosities. Mr. Huskisson has done much in his speech towards preventing the accomplishment of most desirable ends, and should that result, which he has taken for granted will result, from the appointment of the Select Committee, namely, " either an alteration in the law, or the total repeal of the act of last session altogether," a most monstrous evil will be inflicted on the nation.

Mr. Huskisson's speech was made up of complaints and suggestions. The principal of these were :

1. The Committee which sat last year, and recommended the repeal of the laws against combinations, made no report.

2. That the bill went through the house precipitately.

3. That it repealed thirty or forty acts of Parliament.

4. That it set aside the common law.

5. That it induced workmen to think it made combination a duty.

6. That the conduct of workmen was such, " that unless Parliament speedily interfered with some legislative measure to prevent such proceedings from arriving at maturity, his right honourable friend (the home secretary) would ere long have to deal with them in another way, and would have to exert all the civil authority with which he was vested, to protect the property and liberty of the

king's subjects from the formidable conspiracy which appeared organized against them."

1. As to Mr. Huskisson's complaint that the Committee made no report.—This complaint can scarcely be said to have any foundation. The Committee did in fact report, but it put the matter of its report into the form of resolutions, and these resolutions contained the substance of every thing which could have been said in a report; the matter might have been dilated, and spread over many pages of foolscap folio, but it would be difficult for any man to shew that the resolutions were not much better adapted to the purpose than any lengthened formal report could have been. Mr. Huskisson knows well enough that many reports of committees, introductory to minutes of evidence, are neither longer, nor a twentieth part so much to the purpose, as the resolutions he condemns, because they wanted the form of a report; but, when a man has a bad case, and must say something, he is very apt to abandon reasoning, and take to quibbling. So it was with Mr. Huskisson.

The Resolutions of the Committee, so far as they related to the laws against combinations of workmen, were in number eleven. They fairly and impartially stated the case between the masters and the men. They consisted very much of facts fully established by the evidence; such as the partial operation of the laws, the evils they produced, their inadequacy to effect the object aimed at, the acts of violence to which they gave rise, the concurrence of both masters and workmen in the propriety of repealing them, a recommendation to the legislature to repeal them, accompanied by a proposition to enact a summary process for the punishment of those who should use threats, or practise intimidation, or commit violence, on either the property or person of any one. Surely, this was a report not to be found fault with by any reasonable man.

A short account of the Committee and its proceedings will show how carefully the business intrusted to it was managed, how fully it was investigated, and the intense interest a large number of the most enlightened members of the house of commons took in it, previously to their *unanimously* recommending the repeal of the inefficient, vexatious, and noxious laws against combinations of workmen. On the 12th of February, 1824, almost immediately after the meeting of Parliament, Mr. Hume moved for the appointment of the Committee : this was of course with the consent of His Majesty's ministers, or some of them. The Committee, as usual, at first consisted of 21 members ; but such was the desire many members had to understand the whole of this important subject, that they requested to be placed on the Committee, and every one who made the request was placed on the Committee. Twenty-seven gentlemen were thus added to it, and the *Select* Committee consisted of no less than 48 members—a larger number than that which, in the house of commons, frequently deliberates upon—and decides without being unanimous, as the Committee was—the most momentous questions.

Of this Committee, Mr. Hume was the chairman; and he, as chairman, issued a circular note to the mayor, or other head officer, of 40 of the principal cities and towns in the United Kingdom, requesting them to send to the Committee such persons as were competent to give evidence on the business before the Committee: the circular letter was also inserted in the public papers. This was an open, candid, fair, but unusual course: no man can say that notice enough was not given. The Committee sat 36 days, and examined no less than 122 witnesses: these witnesses may be classed as follows, viz.

Members of Parliament	3
Professional and other gentlemen	8
Official ditto	7
Master manufacturers	60
Journeymen	44
	122

It should be observed, that the inquiries of the Committee were directed to the exportation of machinery and the emigration of artizans. But more than 100 of the witnesses were examined as to the effects of the combination laws. The first meeting of the Committee was on the 17th of February, the last on the 22d of May. The

Committee sat for full three months, and examined every person who desired to be examined. This is an extraordinary instance of devotion in a committee of the house of commons, and is quite the reverse of precipitancy.

The circumstances related, were not however the only extraordinary circumstances which attended the proceedings of this Committee; it reported the Minutes of Evidence from time to time to the house of commons; it made no less than six of these Reports, each of which was printed with more than the usual dispatch, and were was very widely distributed; every man who had been, or was to be examined, might have had, and most of them, as well as many other men, and bodies of men, had copies. If, therefore, there ever was a committee which more than another committee, demonstrated their desire for the fullest information; if ever one committee more than any other took the most impartial course, the praise of having done so belongs to this Committee. It must be concluded, that every member of Parliament was well informed on the subject, and was fully prepared to decide on the merits of the case had nothing more been laid before the house at the close of the Committee's labours, than the Minutes of Evidence which had from time to time been printed and distributed. Mr. Huskisson's complaint of the want of a report is not well grounded, and ought to be dismissed.

2. Mr. Huskisson's second head of complaint is, that

the Bill was precipitated through the house. A few words by way of history of the Bill, will serve to shew that there was no hurry in passing it. In the preceding session Mr. Peter Moore brought in " A Bill for repealing several Acts relating to Combinations of Workmen," &c.; and on the 12th of April 1823, Mr. Moore's bill was printed and distributed. This bill of Mr. Moore's recited no less than 45 acts and parts of acts, with a view to their being repealed. Mr. Moore's act contained in substance every thing which the act since passed by the Legislature, and which is now the law of the land, contains. Mr. Moore's bill was largely distributed, and remained for examination and objection from the day it was distributed, during the meeting of Parliament, in which Mr. Moore made several speeches on the subject, and finally it was left for the further consideration of those whom it concerned during the recess; it was thus more than a year before the public, the attention of which had, by discussions in the newspapers, been repeatedly called to the subject. This, with the publicity given by the Committee during three months of the last session, was the very reverse of precipitancy; it was as careful, deliberate, and considerate conduct as it was possible it could be. Finally, the bill was drawn by a gentleman of great respectability and of acknowledged talents, under the sanction of the Attorney General; it was read a first time on the 27th May, and ordered to be printed; read a second time on the 1st of June, committed, amended in the Committee, and ordered to be printed as amended. Reported on the 3d June ; further considered, and re-committed. Again considered in a committee of the whole house on the 4th June, and reported. Read a third time on the 5th June, and passed. Thus the bill was 10 days in the house of commons, was five times brought under the special cognizance of the members, and was twice or thrice amended in the house. It was objected to by no one. Surely the charge of precipitancy can never be admitted against the conduct of the house in respect to this bill ; and thus the second objection must fall to the ground. It is another proof how ill at ease Mr. Huskisson must find himself, when compelled to make such objections; he who knows well what precipitancy really is, and how, on matters of the greatest moment, he and his coadjutors have precipitated bills.

3. Mr. Huskisson's third objection is, that the act repealed 30 or 40 acts of Parliament. This surely is one of its merits. This is a new practice, introduced under the inspection, and with the approbation, of Mr. Huskisson himself, and is a real improvement in our mode of legislating. In the way in which acts of Parliament were formerly drawn, it often became a question, in courts of law, how much of any act was actually repealed ; and it sometimes happened, that both the new law, and the law which it intended to repeal, or some law of equal import with the law which it had repealed, still remained in

force; the one law sometimes directly contradicting the other law, in all such cases embarrassing the Courts, and making the law a snare. The gentleman who drew the bill, has done much towards simplifying and consolidating acts of Parliament; and in this case he seems very wisely to have said, If you mean to repeal the laws which forbid combinations of workmen, you must repeal by name every law and part of every law, in the statute-book, which condemns combinations, or the act will be worse than useless—all such acts and parts of acts were therefore recited, and repealed. Still there was nothing new in this, even as it related to the particular acts repealed, for they had all been inserted by the gentleman before alluded to in Mr. Moore's bill, and had been before the house and the public upwards of twelve months. Mr. Huskisson can hardly be pardoned for making this so proper a proceeding a subject of complaint.

4. Mr. Huskisson's fourth objection is by no means creditable to him. The act, he says, set aside the common law—any thing which should wholly set aside the common law, would confer a blessing on the nation; but, in the present case, Mr. Huskisson uses a form of words to produce effect, when he knows they can answer no other purpose than delusion. What is this common law which Mr. Huskisson, in this instance, brandishes in the faces of his auditors?—what it is, shall be shown;—the

statute of 33 Edward I. A. D. 1305, intituled " *An Or-dinance concerning Conspirators*," is as follows :

" Conspirators be they that do confeder or bind them-selves by oath, covenant, or other alliance, that every of them shall aid and (bear) [sustain the enterprize of] the other falsely and maliciously to indite (or cause to indite) [or cause to be indicted, or falsely to acquit people], or falsly to move or maintain pleas ; and also such as cause children within age to appeal men of felony, whereby they are imprisoned and sore grieved ; and such as maintain men in the country with liveries or fees for to maintain their malicious enterprizes [and to drown the truth], and this extendeth as well to the taken as to the given ; and stewards and bailiffs of great lords, which by their seignory, office, or power, undertake (to bear or maintain quarrels, pleas, or debates, that concern other parties) [to maintain or support pleas or quarrels for parties other] than such as touch the estate of their lords or themselves. This ordinance and final definition of conspirators was made and [finally] accorded by the king and his council [in his Parliament] the thirty-third year of his reign."

This ordinance was made long before laws to prevent combinations of workmen were thought of, and could have no reference to any such circumstance, yet a court of law ruled, that it did apply to combinations of workmen ; and this ruling of the court made it what is called *common law.* By this most wanton and outrageous stretch of power, workmen were placed wholly at the mercy of their employers, who, where they could not or did not choose to prosecute under the laws against combinations, which defined the punishment to be inflicted, and was not therefore in the opinion of some hard-hearted tyrannical men severe enough, they indicted them for conspiracy at the common law. As there was no specific penalty attached to what had been, as has been shown, called common law, the punishment which might be inflicted was wholly at the will of the court, and men were sent to jail for years, for alleged offences which could not have been prosecuted to conviction under the laws against combinations of workmen. To have repealed the laws against combinations, and to have left the working people to the mercy of the misnamed common law, would have been a monstrous absurdity. The false construction of the courts, of the stat. 33 Edw. I. was therefore set aside by the new act, that is, the power of punishing men by the fiction of common law was taken away. It is of this act of justice Mr. Huskisson complains. It is the abolition of this terrible power most shamefully abused which Mr. Huskisson dresses up in words which convey the idea of a monstrously sweeping clause, removing all justice, and giving head to crime; while, as has been explained, it was absolutely necessary, as a mere act of justice, that so pernicious a power should be destroyed.

B

Of the laws against combinations, not one of the witnesses examined before the Committee, in the last session, spoke favourably; one, and one only, wished their continuance on the statute-book; and thus the Committee had the recommendation of the whole body of masters * in favour of the repeal of the laws against combinations, and of course against the false construction of the statute against conspirators, misnamed *common law*.

5. Mr. Huskisson's fifth complaint is, that the law, as it now stands, induces workmen to suppose combination a duty. The law has, however, no such effect on workmen. The laws against their combinations did indeed make them consider it a duty to combine; and it was a duty. Nothing but combination prevented them continually sinking still lower and lower, to the utmost depth the law could sink them; and in as much as they were saved from sinking, they were saved by performing this duty. No fear need be entertained that any combination of workmen will ever be able to keep wages for any considerable time at an exorbitant height. Wages are ultimately regulated by the same laws as profits; and if no mischievous law interferes, both wages and profits will become just what the best interests of the community require they should be. Combinations will occasionally exist,

* Several of the persons examined, represented large bodies of men, as well masters as workmen.

so long as the numbers of workmen are in excess; but they will be divested of their obnoxious character at no distant period, if they be let alone.

Mr. Huskisson talks about combinations, and unions, and constitutions, and delegates, and subscriptions, among workmen, as if they had been all unknown until after the laws against combinations had been repealed. Yet, it is notorious that all ~~these~~ existed during the time the laws against combinations were in force.

Their existence was acknowledged and proved before the Committee, in the last session of Parliament. A detailed account was given of a perpetual organization of many years' standing, which the law had never reached, and was never likely to reach. It was proved in several cases that both masters and men combined, corresponded, ~~subscribed~~, appointed delegates, and raised money by subscriptions. It was proved that both parties habitually broke the laws; and that on some occasions both parties combined together for the very purpose of breaking the law, and ~~thus they~~ acted in open defiance of it. It was proved that the oppression the law occasioned drove men into combinations, and perpetuated them. [It was proved that these combinations were many of them secret combinations, ~~and~~ that these secret combinations sometimes led to conspiracies, and these again were sometimes cemented by illegal oaths. It was repeatedly stated, even by those who were most friendly to coercive measures, that the repeal of the laws against combinations of workmen, would put an end to secret combinations, conspiracies, and illegal oaths.

It was further insisted upon as something more than probable, that if the laws were repealed, the character of combinations would undergo a rapid change, and would in a ~~few~~ few years be wholly divested of their pernicious character and tendency.

Unequal and consequently unjust laws, ~~such as these~~ against combinations of workmen, were the cause of the very evil they were ignorantly ~~supposed~~ to prevent. ~~Men~~ combined ~~against them~~, from a sense of what was called, " a proper pride," from a persuasion that they were more oppressed than they really were ; ~~and~~ men always desire to resist oppression. These, while the laws against combinations of workmen were powerful causes for promoting and perpetuating combinations—these became the bond of union. That bond has been broken by the repeal of the laws against combinations, and none but the most ignorant of mankind can wish to see them restored.

Workmen dread strikes; those who know but little of the habits and circumstances of the working people, talk of strikes as if they were amusements, beneficial amusements; but this is a gross mistake : workmen dread strikes, and well they may : to them a strike, even under favourable circumstances, is a severe punishment; no one ever enters into a strike willingly, every one dreads a repetition. There ~~are~~ in every trade a large number of workmen, whom nothing can ~~ever~~ induce to go heartily into any strike ; many absolutely refuse to strike ; and many desert their fellows when they have struck. When experience shall have shewn, as it will shew, if the men be let alone, that all reasonable and proper objects can be obtained by modes less objectionable, and less injurious to themselves, than those the laws compelled them to resort to, unions, and delegates, and intimidation, and violence, will no longer be heard of. Temporary associations, or combinations, as well of masters as of men, must occasionally take place : many matters can be regulated in no other way, and by no other means ; but, beyond these, there will be very little association of any kind, nothing deserving the name of combination in the sense this word is usually understood.

If keeping down wages, in some cases, by law was a national good,—if the degradation of the whole body of the working people by law was desirable,—if perpetuating discord between masters and workmen was useful,—if litigation was a benefit,—if living in perpetual violation of law was a proper state for workmen and their employers to be placed in, —then the laws against combinations of workmen were good laws, for to all these did they tend.—But if, on the contrary, all these were mischievous results, then were the laws against combinations of workmen bad laws, and the legislature did *acted?* wisely in repealing them. That these were the consequences of the laws, that they were bad laws, and that the legislature acted wisely in repealing them, no man who reads the Minutes of Evidence taken by the Committee of the House of

Commons last session can doubt;* they were proved to be consequences of the law by every one, without a single exception, as well master as man, who was examined before the Committee.

6. Mr. Huskisson's sixth complaint is, that " the spirit of combination has become so prevalent, and threatened property to so great an extent, that, if left to itself, the greatest mischiefs might be apprehended. Unless Parliament speedily interfered with some legislative measure to prevent such proceedings arriving at maturity, his right honourable friend (the home secretary) would ere long have to deal with them in another way, and would have to exert all the civil authority with which he was vested, to protect the property and liberty of His Majesty's subjects from the formidable conspiracy which appeared to be organized against them."—One can hardly persuade one's-self that Mr. Huskisson uttered these words. It might be considered as an error of the reporter, were it not notorious that the *higher classes* have too much the habit of thinking, and sometimes speaking, of the *lower classes,* as persons who have no rights, as outlaws and slaves. The property and liberty of His Majesty's subjects must be protected, aye to be sure, against all foreign enemies, against

---

* See also Mr. White's Digest of the Minutes of Evidence, published by Sherwood, Jones, and Co. Paternoster Row.

all who are not the King's subjects. But did Mr. Huskisson really mean to be understood as implying, that the great body of the people were not the King's subjects? If he uttered the words quoted, he not only represented them as persons " *out of the pale of the constitution*," but as alien enemies of the King, conspirators intent upon destroying the property and liberty of those who are the King's subjects. It is essential to the welfare of society, that the King's subjects should be protected against one another; this is indeed the very end of government: but this is not what Mr. Huskisson has been represented to have said. If this, however, be really what he meant, then it may be replied, that no new laws are necessary: there are laws enough, and punishments severe enough, for those who commit crimes, although it is not always possible to discover the perpetrators. The law which repealed the combination laws, gave to the local magistracy the power to decide, in a summary way, and to punish by imprisonment, persons who committed outrage, or attempted to intimidate others; but as the punishment was severe (two months' imprisonment), it guarded the subject as well as it could from precipitation and injustice—it made two witnesses and two magistrates necessary to a conviction. Of this the people complain: they say, as all appeal is cut off, little regard is paid to the letter of the law; that, as the crime of intimidation is not defined, any thing may be, and sometimes is, called intimidation, and persons are very unjustly punished. They complain of the unnecessary severity of this part of the act. Mr. Huskisson, on the contrary, complains that the law is not severe enough; and that to require two witnesses and two magistrates, is to make conviction unnecessarily difficult; and he is for putting the people more in the power of their employers. It will be difficult, however, to find sound arguments to prove Mr. Huskisson's case. It should be constantly remembered, that this is a new penal enactment; and that the criminal law, in other respects, has not been altered, but may be resorted to at any time. These, as Mr. Huskisson describes them, formidable combinations of workmen, must, he says, be prevented — he will have no combinations of either masters or men. Surely, Mr. Huskisson does not think it possible to prevent combinations by any law, however severe; and no man who has the least claim to the character of a statesman, would ever think combinations could be prevented by act of Parliament; and on the appointment of the Committee on Exportation of Machinery, Mr. Huskisson said, he wished all laws which could not be executed to be repealed.

A law against combination cannot be executed; every such law must in practice be partial, and consequently unjust. It is not possible to contemplate the enactment of more severe laws than those which have been repealed; and yet those laws did not prevent combinations: on the contrary, they perpetuated them, and caused conspiracies and secret oaths. Another evil consequence was, that in those trades which could not, from certain peculiar causes, combine, and perpetually set the law at defiance, wages were reduced to about a third of the amount paid to those trades in which combination, and a constant and habitual disregard of the law, was practised. This is a matter of very great importance; and is a sufficient reason, if no other existed, against any legal interference. But to suppose that combinations among masters could be by law prevented, is to suppose a most gross absurdity. Masters ought to combine, and will combine. No harm, but much good, will in time result from the combinations of both workmen and masters: leave them to themselves; let them alone, until they shall become convinced they must wholly depend upon themselves, and they will then find out the way to accommodate matters. Interfere between them, and they will never be reconciled. Mr. Huskisson may talk as he pleases, may threaten what he pleases;—Mr. Peel may use all the power vested in him;—but all that they, and even an omnipotent Parliament, can do, in the way of compulsion, will produce nothing but mischief. Mr. Huskisson mentioned some cases in which workmen had misconducted themselves: he might have mentioned others; for in several instances workmen have misconducted themselves; but this is no new occurrence. The question which alone deserves to be discussed is, have the evils which existed before ~~the repeal of~~ the laws against combination were repealed, increased or diminished. This the Committee, if its inquiry be as extensive as it ought to be, and as impartial as it ought to be, will ascertain; and the result may confidently be anticipated. More combinations, at least more avowed combinations, exist at the present moment than appeared to exist previous to the repeal of the laws against combinations; but much fewer outrages have been committed than formerly were committed, and these outrages have been openly reprobated by all but those who committed them. In many cases harmony has been restored where discord had long reigned; and evidence is ready to be given, of considerable improvement in the knowledge and dispositions of large masses of the working people, wholly resulting from the facility with which, since the laws against combinations have been repealed, the people have had to associate together. Mr. Huskisson referred to the colliers in certain districts: he showed that their conduct was absurd, but he described it as atrocious; and then, as if conscious of the remedy for the inconvenience which the folly of the men might perhaps occasion, he " recommended those who employed workmen, not to yield, but to meet combination by combination on their part. He was sure, that if they acted with firmness and vigour, and resisted such demands, the magistracy of the country would give them support." No doubt of it; and no doubt this would be found equal to every desirable purpose. In this Mr. Huskisson was himself again:-this is the right way, the only right way, and the only effectual way. If the mode recommended by Mr. Huskisson be adopted, a clear understanding will soon be had, and satisfactory arrangements will soon be made. No parliamentary enactment will accelerate them, but on the contrary every such enactment will retard them.

It is ridiculous to talk of the power of workmen while their numbers are redundant; the masters will always in the end have the advantage, and will be able to punish them. This has been the case already. Mr. Hume, in his reply to Mr. Huskisson, shewed that this had been so in two cases of considerable moment—one in London, the other in Scotland. In Scotland the case is particularly marked, and proves the power wealth possesses over indigence, in the most complete manner. " The first act of combination," said Mr. Hume, " in Glasgow, was the act of the masters. A few men of Mr. Dunlop's manufactory disagreeing with their master, he believed on some point of wages, they declined to continue working for him. What was the consequence? Why the masters immediately combined together; for they called a meeting at which the subject was discussed, when they came to a resolution to make a stand against the men : this they effected in the following manner. They published a notice, stating, that ' if the men of Mr. Dunlop's factory did not return to their work on or before the Monday morning next, they (the masters) would discharge from their employ all the men, amounting in number to ten thousand, until the men who had quitted Mr. Dunlop returned to him.' The workmen who had gone away, disclaimed acting in concert with the others, and said, ' Do not punish them for what we have done.' Their disclaimer was not attended to,

and all the men in Glasgow, in the same trade, were actually
turned out of employment. Now he would ask, whether the
mere declining to work for Mr. Dunlop was to be put in
comparison, for enormity, with that act of the masters. But
that was not all : the property of the masters enabled them to
get the better of the men, who were at last obliged to come
in unconditionally. When they did so, the masters punished
them again in a most decided manner; for they actually de-
ducted for the loss they had sustained by their own act in
stopping their mills, from the amount of the men's wages;
compelling them to pay ten per cent. from their wages
weekly; and this was to continue until the masters should be
satisfied."—This shows with whom is the power. The
men may occasionally, in their attempts to prevent degradation, cause some embarrassment to their employers;
but so long as the number of hands continue to be greater

than is necessary to perform all the labour required,
so long will the power of control, aye and of oppression too,
be held by the masters. Mr. Huskisson recommended the
masters to combine: he may be assured that they are combined in numberless instances, that they know their power,
and will continue to combine, for the purpose of exercising
it, until a better understanding shall take place. They need
no law still further to enable them to commit extensive acts
of oppression. So far was this power recently carried in
Glasgow, so openly was it exercised, so great was the evil
inflicted on the working people, that many, very many re-

spectable persons subscribed both money and food to keep
the people from starving. The theatre at Glasgow was
opened for their relief, and the net proceeds are stated at
upwards of £80 — a large sum to be thus collected. The
playhouse must have been filled, not with poor operatives,
but with respectable people, who, had they not commise-
rated the case of the workmen, would not have paid money
for admission to assist and support them against the oppression and cruelty of their masters. Another proof of the abso-
lute power of the masters, and the want of means of protecting themselves, is exhibited in the conduct of the owners of
cotton mills in the county of Lancaster, both before and
since the combination laws were repealed : men and women
who offended their employers, no matter from what cause,
were proscribed by the masters, and expelled the trade : many
have been several years unable to get a day's employment in any mill. I have now before me three printed lists,
copies of those sent round by certain masters at Hyde and
Stockport only (since the repeal of the laws against combinations), containing the names of *two hundred and three* proscribed men and women, and the names of the masters who
have proscribed them. Surely, no more power than this is
necessary. The power to proscribe and thus to starve people
in large numbers, is surely sufficient. Workmen, however,
ask no law to stay this evil, because they know well enough
that no law can prevent it; but the masters do not think this
power enough, and they demand more. Let us hope the

legislature will leave these matters to time, and not, by med-
dling, make them worse. No law can remedy the inconveniences which must occasionally occur—no law is necessary
to punish violence—violence may be punished by existing
laws—if let alone, little violence will take place—make a law
on the subject, and discontent and violence will increase.
The evils occasioned by the laws against combinations, are
rapidly declining; satisfactory arrangements have been made
in many places between masters and men, which never could
have been made under the old laws; and if government
cease to agitate the question, and leave the masters and men
to themselves, these arrangements will become general. The
people begin to see, that the cause of their ignorance and
degradation is the redundancy of numbers pushing one another out, and underselling one another; and this knowledge,
of such vast importance to them, will, when it becomes
general, prevent them from attributing their degradation to
wrong causes, and seeking hopeless remedies by annoying
their employers.

This may be illustrated most perfectly by the case of Mr.
Dunlop. Such was the vexation and disorder, so prevalent
was violence and threats of violence some years ago, that Mr.
Dunlop, with the whole of the " between 30 and 40 acts of
Parliament," which have since been repealed to assist him,
aye, and with the " common law " at his back, he either was,
or pretended to be, so alarmed at the want of protection
the law, statute and common, afforded him, that he took

away a portion of his capital, and established a cotton mill in
a foreign country, where of course the laws gave him the
protection, which " between 30 and 40 acts of Parliament
and the common law" could not give him in Great Britain.
He sought protection for his property in North America,
where not a single law, statute or common, made combinations of workmen a crime; where wages, as he himself told
the Committee of the House of Commons, were as 40 to 25
in Glasgow,—three-fifths higher in America than in Glasgow.
The machinery in Glasgow was, he said, superior to that in
America; the goods produced in Glasgow were better than
those produced in America; and yet it answered his purpose
to establish a cotton manufactory there.

The case which seemed to be by far the most reprehensible
was, the attempt of the operatives in Glasgow to " root out"
Mr. Hutcheson. This, as it well might, excited great attention and equal detestation. The attempt totally, and for
ever, to prevent a large and respectable manufacturer from
ever having a workman, was equally silly and atrocious, and
was met as all such attempts ought to have been met. It is
the last attempt of the kind that will ever be made; the
ignorance as well as the injustice of that attempt has been
manifested, and it will be impossible again to induce a large
body of men to commit such an extravagance. But even here
it seems the operatives were imposed upon and misled by the
masters. Mr. Hutcheson has himself declared, that the attempt did not originate with the workmen, but that they were

set on by the manufacturers, his competitors, who intimated to the men, that their wages would never be raised unless they rooted him out of the trade.—Not one word of comment on this can be necessary.

These transactions are conclusive, both as to causes and remedies; they are alone sufficient to induce reasonable men to cease interfering in trading concerns between workmen and their employers.

Mr. Huskisson's speech has agitated the working people all over the kingdom. They are, however, ready and willing to have their conduct thoroughly investigated; and if the Committee, following the example set by the Committee in the last session, will but give them a full and patient hearing, they will make such a case as cannot fail to convince every unprejudiced man, that the repeal of the combination laws has already conferred a great blessing on them ; has led, and will continue to lead, to a state of things equally beneficial to them and to the nation.

F. P.

April 23d, 1825.

J. Innes, Printer, 61, *Wells-street, Oxford-street, London.*

Combinations of Workmen.

SUBSTANCE

OF THE

SPEECH

OF

FRANCIS JEFFREY, Esq.

UPON INTRODUCING THE TOAST,

" *Freedom of Labour—But let the Labourer recollect, that in exercising his own rights, he cannot be permitted to violate the rights of others.* "

AT THE

PUBLIC DINNER GIVEN AT EDINBURGH

TO

JOSEPH HUME, Esq. M. P.

ON FRIDAY THE 18TH OF NOVEMBER 1825.

PUBLISHED AT THE REQUEST OF THE MEETING.

EDINBURGH:

PRINTED FOR ARCHIBALD CONSTABLE AND COMPANY, EDINBURGH; HURST, ROBINSON AND COMPANY, LONDON; AND SOLD BY ALL THE BOOKSELLERS IN LONDON, GLASGOW, LEEDS, MANCHESTER, BIRMINGHAM, SHEFFIELD, ABERDEEN, DUBLIN, NEWCASTLE-ON-TYNE, PERTH, DUNDEE, NEWCASTLE, HULL, AND LIVERPOOL.

1825.

SPEECH, &c.

I wish now, Sir, with your permission, to propose a toast, which, though the subject has been already alluded to in the course of the evening, I think it would be unfit to leave out on this occasion—although I feel that, in the present state of the country, it cannot be proposed without some explanation—and even perhaps some mixture of discordant and opposite feelings.

From the few words I have already uttered, you may perhaps have conjectured that it relates to the recent abolition of the Laws against Combination among workmen—effected mainly by the talents and perseverance of the distinguished Individual beside you—and to the disorders which have unfortunately since taken place, in various parts of the country, among that class of the population.

Not many months ago, Mr Hume's success in this great measure was hailed by his friends as

one of the happiest and most beneficial of his
many triumphs ; and I really do not recollect
any instance in which right thinking men of all
parties, seemed more heartily to concur, than in
applauding the vigour, the prudence, the patience and perseverance by which he had at
last succeeded, against old and powerful prejudices, in extending the great principle of *free
competition* to the great market of Labour, and
relieving the labourer, in the disposal of this
his only property, from the irritating, unequal,
and degrading restrictions of the Laws against
Combination.

Subsequent events, it cannot be dissembled,
have something disturbed this unanimity; and
while they have most sensibly afflicted and
mortified those who hold firmly to the principle, have given but too much appearance of
triumph to those who are opposed to it ; and,
what is infinitely more to be lamented, have
led many good, sensible, and liberal men to en-
tertain serious doubts of the policy or safety of
the measures which have been lately adopted.—
Of that number, Sir, certainly I am *not* one. I
think quite as well of the cause in which that
battle was fought and won, and quite as highly (nay more highly) of the merits of the lead-
er under whose auspices it was won, as before any of those, for whose sake it was risked,
had proceeded to abuse the victory. And

though there are individuals beyond all doubt deserving the severest reprobation, I cannot but think, that by far the greater part of the evils to which I refer, are to be ascribed, not to *the abolition* of the Combination Laws, but to the delusive opinions, and, above all, to the bad spirit which had been engendered by their previous *existence.*

These laws, Sir, I am firmly and deeply convinced, were fundamentally Unjust in their principle, and Mischievous in their practical operation. It is but fair however to state, that the *mischief,* in my opinion, was far greater than the *injustice.* I do not myself believe that they enabled masters to keep the wages of their workmen, permanently or systematically, below their proper level; but they produced an universal *opinion* to that effect among the workmen; and fostered all the bad passions and unhappy propensities that naturally sprung from that opinion. Their great evil was, not that they kept wages unreasonably low, but that they made every variation in their rate, an occasion of hostility, suspicion, and disorder; and kept up a perpetual ferment and spirit of animosity among those whose interests were in truth inseparable, and upon whose cordial cooperation, not only their own prosperity, but the peace and the happiness of the community depended.

I do not mean, however, to deny, that they were also substantially unjust; and that they did expose the workmen to disadvantage, by *obstructing* and *retarding*, in many cases, that fair settlement and adjustment of their mutual pretensions, which, though it could not be ultimately prevented, either by combinations, or laws against combination—certainly was not likely to be so soon, or so comfortably accomplished, where the parties were not upon equal terms, as to the freedom and authority with which they were enabled to state them. Understanding that it amounted to Combination—and it was so held in law—for a multitude of workmen to consult together as to the proper rate of wages for which they should insist, and, on this being refused, to leave their employment in great numbers at once—I have no hesitation in saying, that it was palpably *unjust* to prohibit *such* combinations; and that, without being allowed to enter into them, workmen might often be subjected to great temporary disadvantage, and both they and their masters kept hurtfully in the dark, as to the true measure of their just claims on each other. A single master was at liberty, at any time, to turn off *the whole* of his workmen at once,—100 or 1000 in number—if they would not accept of the wages he chose to offer. But it was made an offence for the whole of the workmen to leave that master at once, if he refused to give the wages they chose to require! It is evident, that in this there was no equality or fairness. By interdicting such combinations, the workmen were prevented, when deliberating on by far the most important of their concerns, from availing themselves of the collective knowledge, prudence, and experience of the whole body ; and, at the same time, from stating the result of their consultations with that effect and authority, which must always belong to the concurring opinions of men resolving after full deliberation. In the natural course of things, and when men's minds have not been inflamed by accidental causes, the effect of such concert and consultation must generally be, to allay the impatience of the rash and ignorant by the caution and experience of the better instructed, and to prevent, rather than to urge on, extravagant and unreasonable pretensions ; while it must obviously give weight to all just and fair proposals, and ensure a serious and careful consideration of reasons, which might not have obtained a hearing in the mouths of insulated individuals.

For these, and other reasons, I think the principle of the Combination Laws was unjust ; and have no doubt, that it was a deep and instinctive sense of this injustice, that led to all those indirect and practical effects which constituted

by far the greatest part of their evil. In the *first*
place, it led unavoidably to *secret* and *concealed*,
instead of open and avowed deliberations ; and
by a necessary and immediate consequence to
all the vices and abuses which are inseparable
from disguise and concealment. Men, meeting in
conscious violation of the law, are speedily in-
fected with the spirit and the desperation of
outlaws; and are in imminent hazard of having
their original objects extended or perverted to
others of a far more dangerous description ;
while the punishment, with which they are occasionally visited, only exasperates still more
strongly their feeling of injustice, embitters
more deeply their animosity towards their opponents, and rivets more firmly the erroneous
conviction, that it is by these restraints alone that
they are prevented from greatly bettering their
condition.

It is needless, however, I am persuaded, to
say more upon this view of the subject. The
truths, to which I have now very generally alluded, were established in the Committees of Parliament, to the complete conviction of many who
had entered upon the inquiry with the strongest prepossessions against them ; and, by an
overwhelming weight of testimony, derived almost entirely from the most experienced and
extensive MASTER manufacturers in the kingdom. A very great number, I believe not less

than seventy or eighty, persons of this description were examined on these occasions; and, with
an unanimity altogether surprising on such a
question,—interrupted by the dissent of but six
or seven, I think, out of the whole number,—
testified most decidedly, both as to the utter in-
efficiency of the Combination Laws to prevent
any disorder, and as to the infinite mischief and
discomfort that resulted from their indirect operation.

I confidently trust, therefore, that whatever
remedies may be suggested for the disorders
which are said to have resulted from their abolition, it will never be seriously proposed to re-
enact them—the truth being, that they had
been all along the feeding root and cause of
those very disorders—and that their germs were
to be found exclusively in the shallow and unjust
policy which has now been deliberately abandoned.

In glancing, for a moment, at the evidence
of this assertion, I must beg leave to distinguish the merely *extravagant* and *unreasonable*
part of the proceedings which have lately excited so much alarm, from the *guilty* and reprehensible parts. The former, I think, all
men who have an ordinary knowledge of human nature, and of the previous state of the
parties, must have expected and been prepared
to endure. The latter has come upon most of

us certainly with a very painful surprise, and
ought no more to be endured, than it could have
been reasonably anticipated :—at the same time
that it is evident, on a little reflection, that *the extent* and *malignity* of the evil, is to be ascribed
chiefly to that excited state of mind, and to
the prevalence of those extravagant hopes and
erroneous opinions, which, by involving men in
disappointment and delusion, exposed them so
peculiarly to the temptations to guilt.

To a certain extent, it was manifest that
men newly admitted to the exercise of a privilege to which, while withheld from them, they
had attached an exaggerated importance, would
be both unreasonably eager to proceed to the
exercise of it, and unreasonably mortified to
find that it produced no very considerable effects.
They naturally, though most erroneously, believed, that it was in a great measure by the restraints upon their combining, and by permitted combinations among their masters, that
their wages had been kept down—and had little doubt that, if they could only reverse the
talisman, now that it was placed in their hands,
they might immediately effect a prodigious improvement in their condition. They combined, therefore, in a great variety of cases, where
there was no need for combination—demanded
extravagant rates of wages, where they were
already as high as could be afforded—and de-

serted their work when it was utterly impossible that they could ever be bribed back to it by any advance on their former emoluments. These proceedings occasioned great embarrassment, no doubt, and much loss and distress, both to the workmen and their employers. On this account, they were exceedingly to be lamented—and to be repressed by every possible resource of remonstrance, expostulation, reasoning, and conciliation. But they did not justify any higher or harsher remedies. They were not in themselves illegal; and had nothing criminal, or even blameworthy, in their motives. The persons who betook themselves to them were sure to be the greatest sufferers—and, above all, it was certain that, by their very sufferings, they must soon be convinced of their error, and deterred, most probably, from ever venturing on their repetition. They were the errors of inexperience and ignorance ; and led directly to their own cure. They were the natural accompaniments of a change from restraint to indulgence ; and were sure to pass away, like a summer storm on the breaking up of the bad weather. They were not the symptoms of any permanent distemper in the body of our labouring population, but merely of the *seasoning fever* of men new to the climate of liberty.

For this class of disorders, therefore, for these

excesses, rather than abuses of the freedom so suddenly conferred on them, I think we should feel the greatest possible indulgence, and the least possible alarm. They are exactly what might have been foreseen, and what, with an ordinary degree of patience and management, we may be sure will speedily disappear. The true cure and preventive for the errors in which they originate, is to be found in those plain and simple doctrines of Political Economy, which explain the dependence of the rate of wages *on the proportion* which the number of labourers in any country bears to the quantity of capital which has been accumulated in it for their support—and demonstrate the utter *impossibility* of any set of labourers permanently getting either more or less than their fair share of it, by any contrivance whatever—and the perfect inefficacy of combination to increase this share. Into those doctrines it would be absurd for me to think of entering on such an occasion as this ; but while I am perfectly satisfied that, by friendly and patient explanation, they may be made clear and intelligible to the great bulk of our labourers, and that no one who has frequent opportunities of meeting with them, can be so well employed as in earnestly inculcating them on their understandings, there are one or two suggestions, of a very plain and conclusive nature, which I am tempted to take this opportunity of throwing out for their consideration.

I would beg leave, for instance, to suggest, in the *first* place, that as combinations and cessation of work cannot possibly increase the wealth or capital of the country, but, on the contrary, must evidently diminish it, their effect must be to leave less, and not more, funds for the maintenance of labour than previously existed.

Secondly, I would suggest that, if a rise of wages is obtained in any employment, this must necessarily diminish the profits of the masters; and these masters will consequently be tempted to give up that employment, and withdraw their capital to some other; from which it cannot but result, that there will be less employment for the labourers who remain in it, and their wages, from their competition for that employment, will unavoidably fall much lower than they were when they first combined to raise them.

Thirdly, I would suggest that, if they should, by the use of this sort of compulsion, extort, for a time, higher wages than were paid in other branches of industry, the consequence would infallibly be, that labourers would speedily flock from those other branches, to share in those high wages, and, by their competition, would speedily bid them down, below even their original level.

Fourthly, I would suggest, that long-conti-
nued combinations must always afford evidence
of the non-existence of that pretended necessity for an advance of rates, by which alone
they could ever be justified. For, if large bodies of workmen can maintain themselves in
idleness for any considerable time, on the savings of their former wages—or, as is now more
common, can be so maintained by contributions voluntarily saved out of what are called
the low and inadequate wages earned by other
workmen, it must be commonly thought that
the wages which can afford so large a surplus,
after maintaining the actual labourers, cannot
be so very low.

Finally, I would beg leave to suggest, (what
I found the other day in a paper sent to me ano-
nymously), that it would be of infinite advantage to the workmen, both as giving efficacy to
such occasional combinations as may be necessary, and as preventing that necessity by the
perpetual presence of an effectual check to injustice on either side, if workmen would generally instruct themselves in the exercise of
more than one trade, or branch of industry.
In all the simpler and most numerous branches, this might be effected, I am persuaded, with the greatest facility ; and the result
would be, that when a workman left one occupation, from a conviction that the wages in it
were below the proper or general standard, he

could scarcely fail, if that were the fact, to find more advantageous employment in that other to which he might then at once betake himself; while, on the other hand, if a master was left by his workmen, combining to ask what was really too high a rate of wages, he might *instantly* supply their places with other skilled workmen, whom a very slight and temporary advance would immediately draw from their actual employments. In this way, it appears to me, that, by the free circulation of *labour* from one occupation to another, its wages would be at all times equalized, and maintained at their proper level—just as, by a similar circulation of *capital*, the *profits* on it are, in all well peopled countries, equalized in all its different occupations.

By those, and by such considerations, which I am confident may be made quite level to the comprehension of most of our workmen, the restoration of many who are now wasting their little savings in unprofitable idleness—losing their habits of contented industry and domestic independence—and fostering groundless and pernicious animosities towards those with whom they should be cordially united—might be accelerated and secured, and many others prevented from entering upon the same ruinous and unhappy career.

Of these deluded persons I would speak, as I

am sure I feel, with the most affectionate indulgence and the kindest consideration; and think
no efforts irksome, and no labour too great,
that promised to bring them back in safety
from the perilous courses on which they have
lately adventured. But there is another description of persons, and a different sort of adven-
ture, of which it is impossible to think or to
speak with any such feelings. Those persons I
mean, who, not contented with using to its utmost extent the liberty of combining, and of
leaving their employments in concert, which
the law has lately allowed them, have proceeded to acts of the most lawless violence, intimidation, and outrage,—not only against their employers, whose wages they have refused—but
against such of their fellow labourers as are
still contented to work for these wages. For
such persons and such proceedings, I think
there should be *no indulgence* and *no toleration ;*
and that those who are most friendly to the
rights and interests of the lower orders should
be the first and most forward to mark them with
their unmeasured reprobation.

I trust the number, with whom the guilt of
those most criminal proceedings will ultimately
rest, may turn out to be but small. I believe,
and it is my comfort to believe, that they have
originated with a few distempered and discon-
tented spirits, who have been enabled, by the ge-

neral inflammable and excited state of the workmen's minds, for which I have already endea-
voured to account, to produce an effect upon
many of them, which, in a calmer season, they
would have attempted in vain. I am not without
my suspicions, that advantage has also been taken
of that excitement, by interested and malignant
individuals, to fan these embers of discontent,
by their incendiary arts, into a destructive flame.
There are pregnant grounds, I have understood,
in some quarters at least, for such a suspicion;
and I hope and trust that they will be jealously
and vigilantly investigated. But on whomsoever
the guilt of originating these outrages may ultimately attach, I cannot but say that it is a
guilt, in my eyes, of the most atrocious and re-
volting character—and has on it all the aggra-
vations that can belong to any act of personal
cruelty, depredation, and baseness.

It is marked, in the *first* place, by the most
gross and glaring *inconsistency* between the objects they profess to pursue, and the unhallow-
ed means by which they seek to attain them.
They are asserting, it seems, their right to the
free disposal of their labour; and their first step
is to impose on all around them the most tyrannical and sanguinary restraint! They have just
been emancipated from the bondage of those
laws which obstructed in some degree their
just liberty of working or refusing to work as

B

they themselves might think fit; and which they have never ceased to denounce as odious, for subjecting them to some risk of some moderate punishment, for concerting with each other as to the best way of asserting that liberty—and now, they tell such of their fellows as do not agree in their opinions, that *they shall have no liberty* to work or refuse work, except as they are directed by them! and proceed to prohibit—not by the fear of a few months imprisonment, openly inflicted by the reluctant severity of the law, but by the fear or the certainty of lawless and sanguinary violence,—of midnight assaults, arsons and murder,—vast multitudes of their brethern from accepting the wages with which they are perfectly contented, and by the cessation of which, even for a day, they and their families may be plunged in irremediable ruin!

It has on it, besides, the stamp of the two most hateful and degrading attributes of human corruption—the twin vices of cowardice and cruelty. It attacks the poor, the few, the unprepared, the defenceless!—it skulks in darkness and in corners; and seeks to encourage itself by the array, and to shelter itself in the confusion, of disorderly multitudes!

For actions that bear such a character, there is no palliation to be found, in the wretchedness of those who commit them—no ground of appealing to our sympathy, on the score of their being done in the too eager pursuit of their own relief from poverty and degradation. Least of all can they hope that such apologies can ever be listened to by the sincere friends of the lower orders,—by those who are desirous, above all things, of the happiness, respectability, and independence of the working classes. For the worst and most fatal aggravation of the crimes of which I have been speaking, is, that they tend to bring disgrace and discredit on the whole of those important classes ; and expose millions of deserving individuals to the imminent hazard of having their hard-won liberties again taken away, for the guilt and misconduct of a few thousand undeservers. I have already said, and every one that lives in society must be aware of the fact, that the frequency and extent of the shameful outrages to which I have alluded, have so much disgusted and alarmed many good and reasonable men, as to make them doubt of the policy of the late abolition of the laws against combination, and to lend no unfavourable ear to the suggestions which are so eagerly made for their reenactment, as to make them fear, in short, they had judged too favourably of the sense and virtue of the lower orders in general, and almost to make them believe that they are still unfit to be trusted with what cannot be denied to be their rights.

For my own part, I cannot part so easily with

opinions that are so necessary to my comfort, and to all my happy anticipations for my country. I believe that this crisis is but temporary —that the authors of the criminal acts that disgrace it are but few—and that their influence arises altogether from the transitory excitement which is inseparable from the newness of liberty, and cannot continue long after it has become familiar. But I can have no assurance that this will be the belief or opinion of the Legislature, or the majority of the country; and it is impossible to deny, that a little longer continuance, and a little greater excess of these disorders, will make it difficult for *any one* to maintain this belief, or adhere to these opinions.

The independence or degradation of the lower orders now depends, therefore, on their own conduct. If there are to be restraints on the freedom of labour, it is unquestionably better that they should be enforced by law, than by the violence of a brutal and sanguinary rabble; and, if the great body of our workmen are not disposed to allow this freedom *to each other*, it is plain that they have no right to claim it for *themselves*. I trust, however, that they will no longer delay to assert what I still believe to be their true character; and will make good their claim to the continuance of the privileges they have obtained, by separating themselves, at once and for ever, from all those associations

that have polluted themselves by base and un-
manly crimes, or interfered, by intimidation
and outrage, with the free industry of their defenceless fellows. If they do not,—it is sicken-
ing to think what evils they are preparing for
themselves : For, whatever some of them may
now think, the truth undoubtedly is, that no
tyrannical master, or combination of masters,
could ever do them one thousandth part of the
mischief which they will then have to suffer for
the acts of these rioters and depredators—
their most fatal and intestine enemies !

I am afraid, Sir, that I have detained you a
great deal too long on this subject—not indeed
in respect of its importance, but with a view to
the little value of the remarks I have made on
it, and to the nature of the meeting, on whose
patience I have trespassed with them. My
mind, however, was full of the subject—and I
will confess that I am sanguine enough to hope
that some effect may be produced, even on the
misguided individuals of whom I have been
speaking, by a public and decided statement of
these opinions on this particular occasion. That
prejudices should exist *against* the rightful
claims of the lower orders, in a meeting of the
friends of Mr Hume, no incendiary even will
ever persuade them to believe. The place in
which I have uttered these sentiments—the
presence in which I have uttered them, and the

warmth and cordiality with which they have
now been received, must, I think, satisfy all to
whom any report of them may come, that they
proceed at least from no unfriendly adviser :—
And, perhaps, I may be permitted to add, that
the life and character of the individual, from
whose lips they proceed, may be accepted as
some pledge, both of their kindness and their
sincerity. If it were possible to imagine that
any jealousy of popular rights, any idle dread
of popular excesses, any indifference to the
sufferings of the people, in short, or any re-
verence for their oppressors, should exist in
such an assembly, I think I may say, that
the people of Scotland would not readily believe that *I* should voluntarily stand forward
as the advocate of such opinions. To promote
the happiness, and advance the condition of the
lower orders, has been one great object of my
life—and I do not hesitate to say, that the immediate sufferings that must wait on the crimes
of which I have been speaking, seem to me a
far less evil than the permanent degradation to
which they threaten to sink so large a portion
of the people. It is for the sake of their future
freedom—more even than for their present comfort and safety—that I now warn them against
these contagious and most guilty excesses ; and
implore them to abstain from forfeiting their

own liberty by invading that of their neigh-
bours.

I beg leave to give as my toast, " Freedom
of Labour—But let the Labourer recollect,
that in exercising his own rights, he cannot be
permitted to violate the rights of others. "

Printed by J. Hutchison,
for the Heirs of D. Willison.

British Labour Struggles:
Contemporary Pamphlets 1727-1850

An Arno Press/New York Times Collection

The Factory Act of 1833. 1833-1834.

Richard Oastler: King of Factory Children. 1835-1861.

The Battle for the Ten Hours Day Continues. 1837-1843.

The Factory Education Bill of 1843. 1843.

Prelude to Victory of the Ten Hours Movement. 1844.

Sunday Work. 1794-1856.

Demands for Early Closing Hours. 1843.

Conditions of Work and Living: The Reawakening of the English Conscience. 1838-1844.

Improving the Lot of the Chimney Sweeps. 1785-1840.

The Rising of the Agricultural Labourers. 1830-1831.

The Aftermath of the "Lost Labourers' Revolt". 1830-1831.